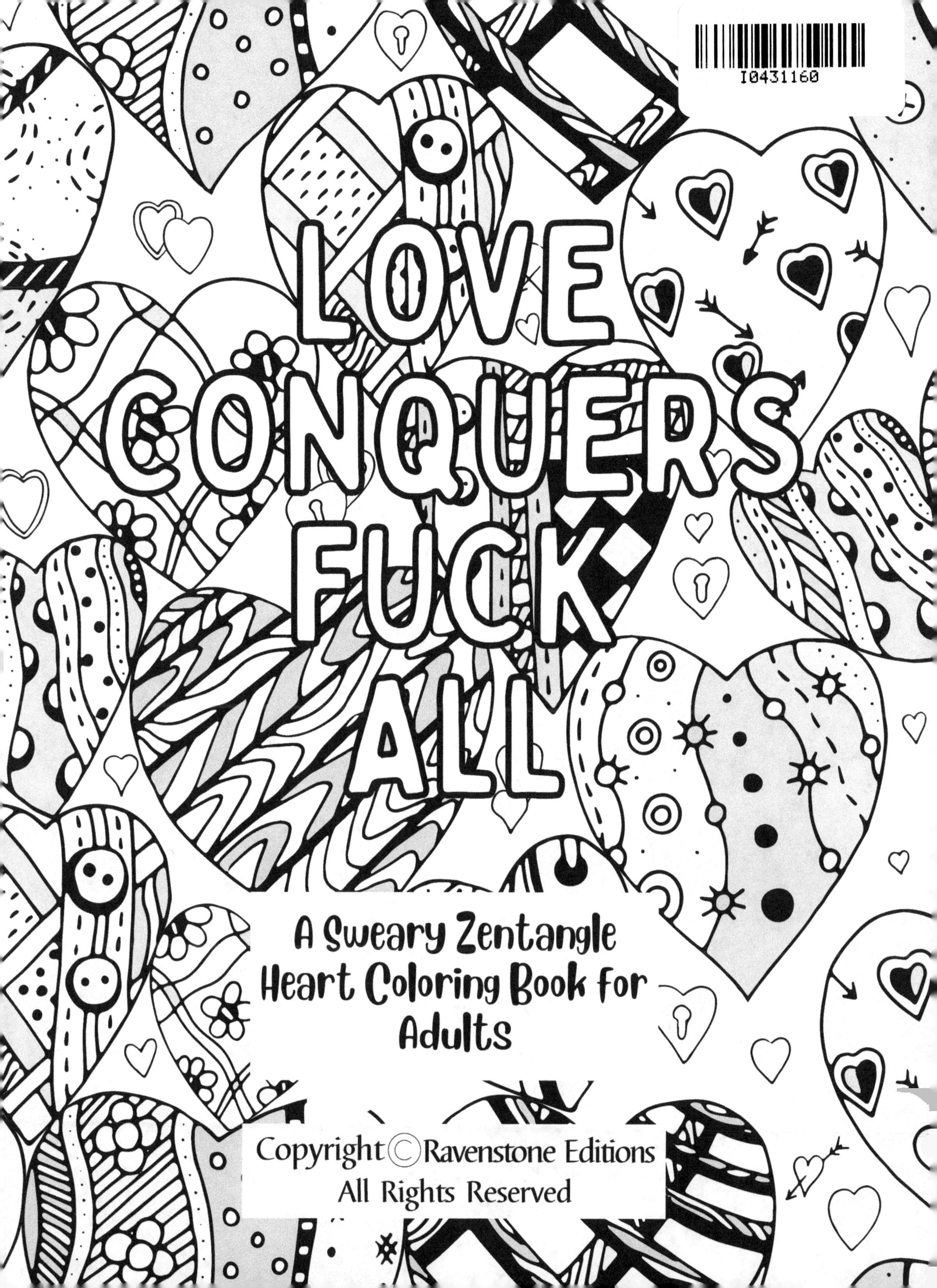

LOVE CONQUERS FUCK ALL

A Sweary Zentangle Heart Coloring Book For Adults

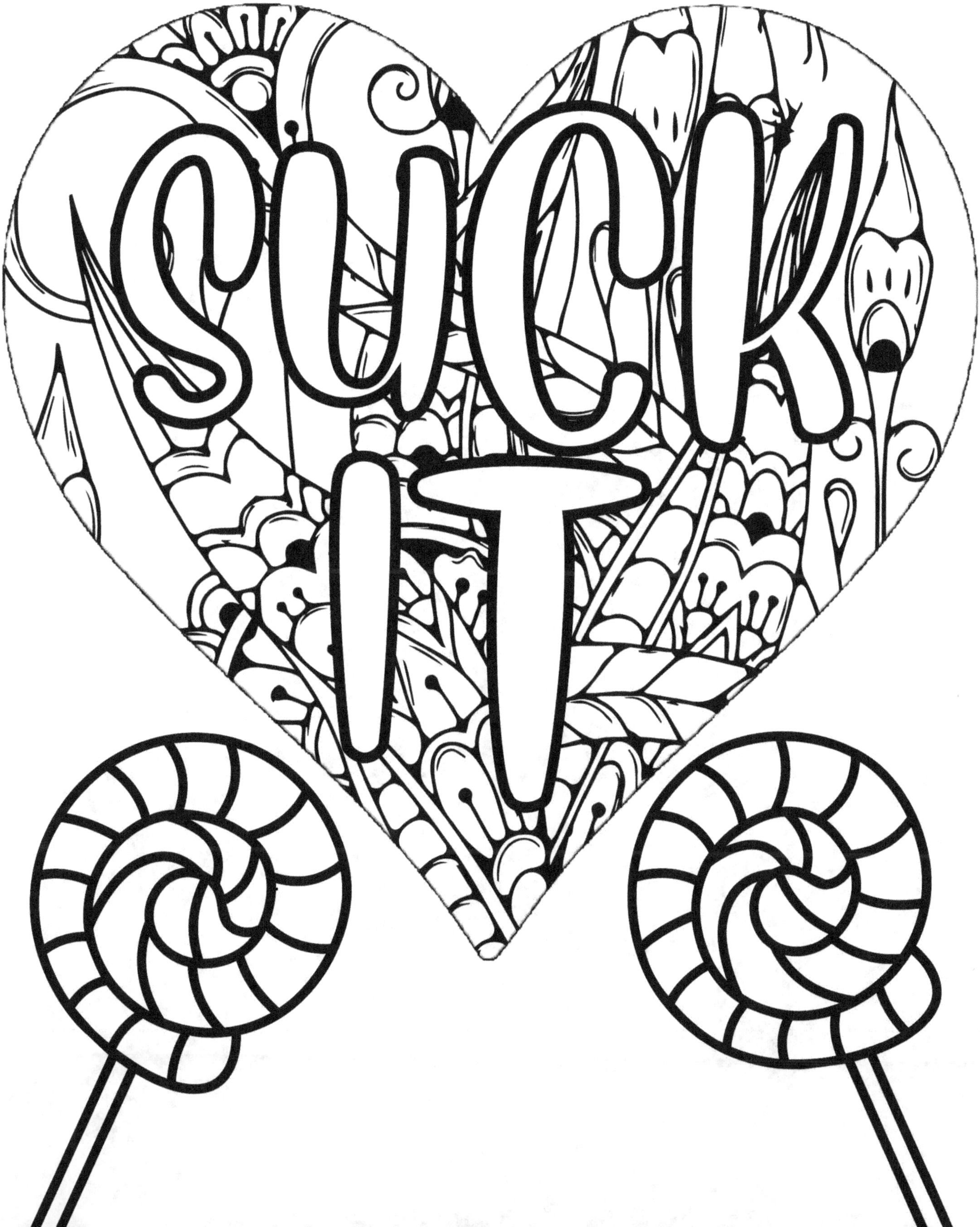
SUCK
IT

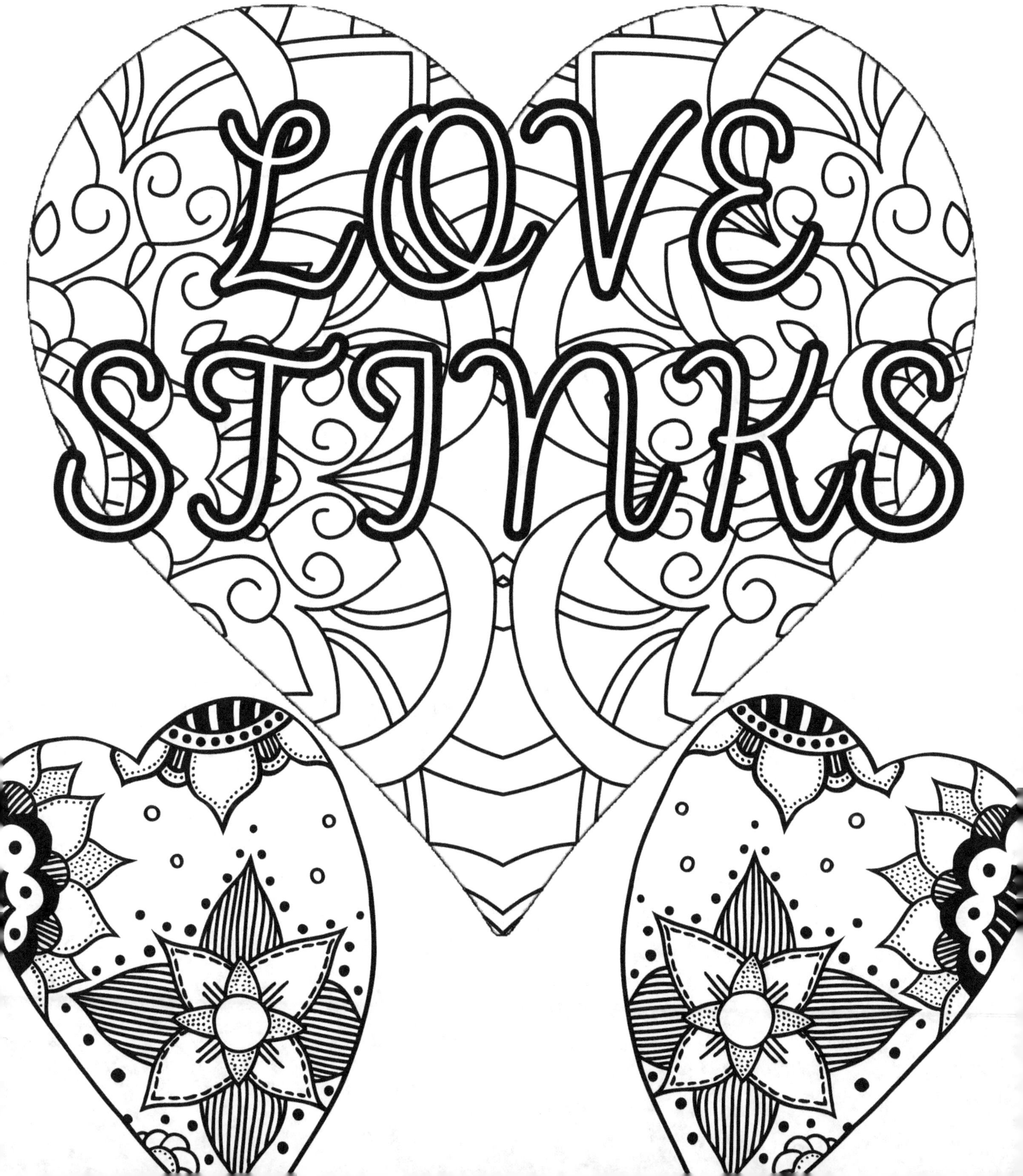
LOVE
STINKS

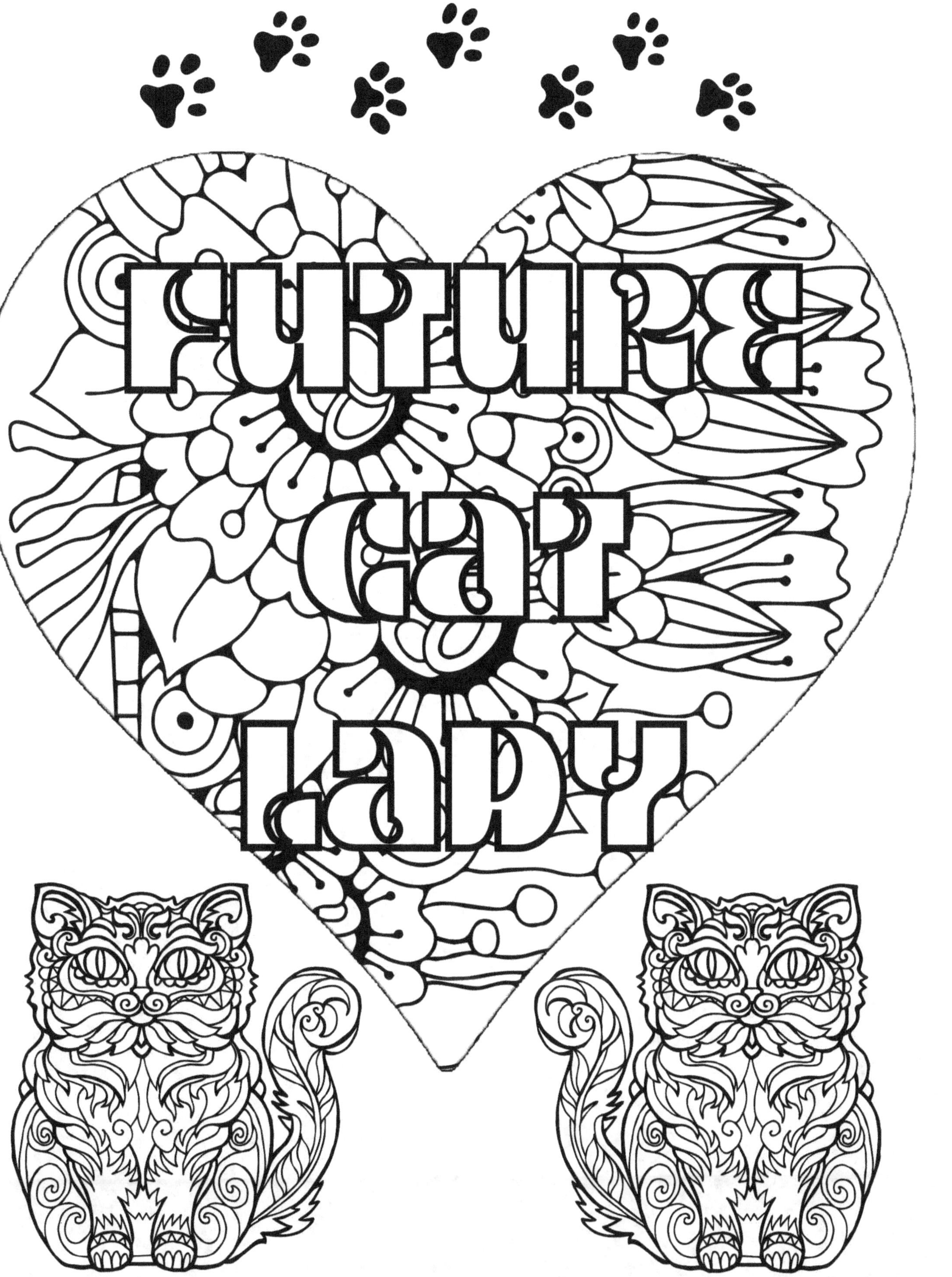
FUTURE
CAT
LADY

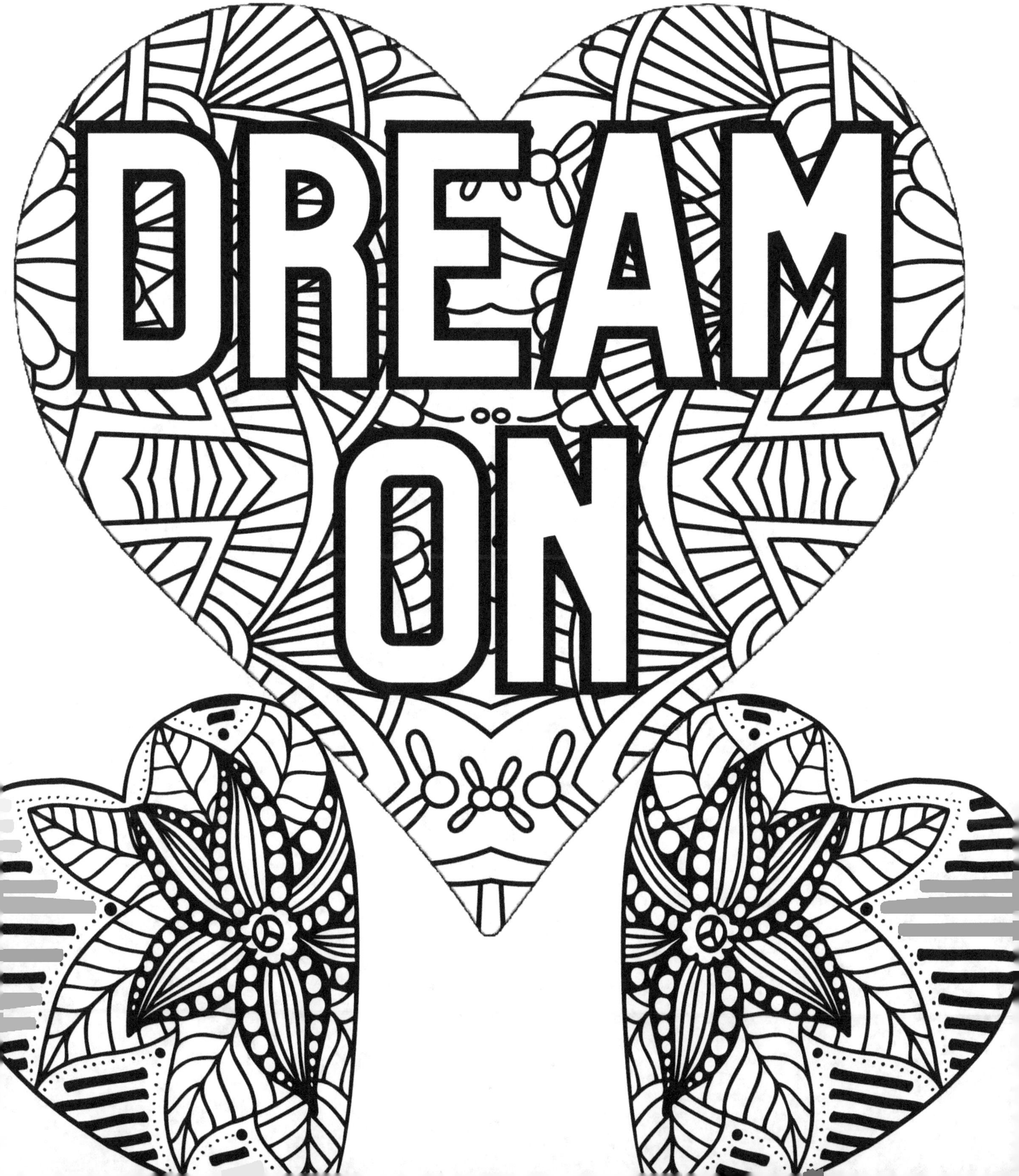
DREAM
ON

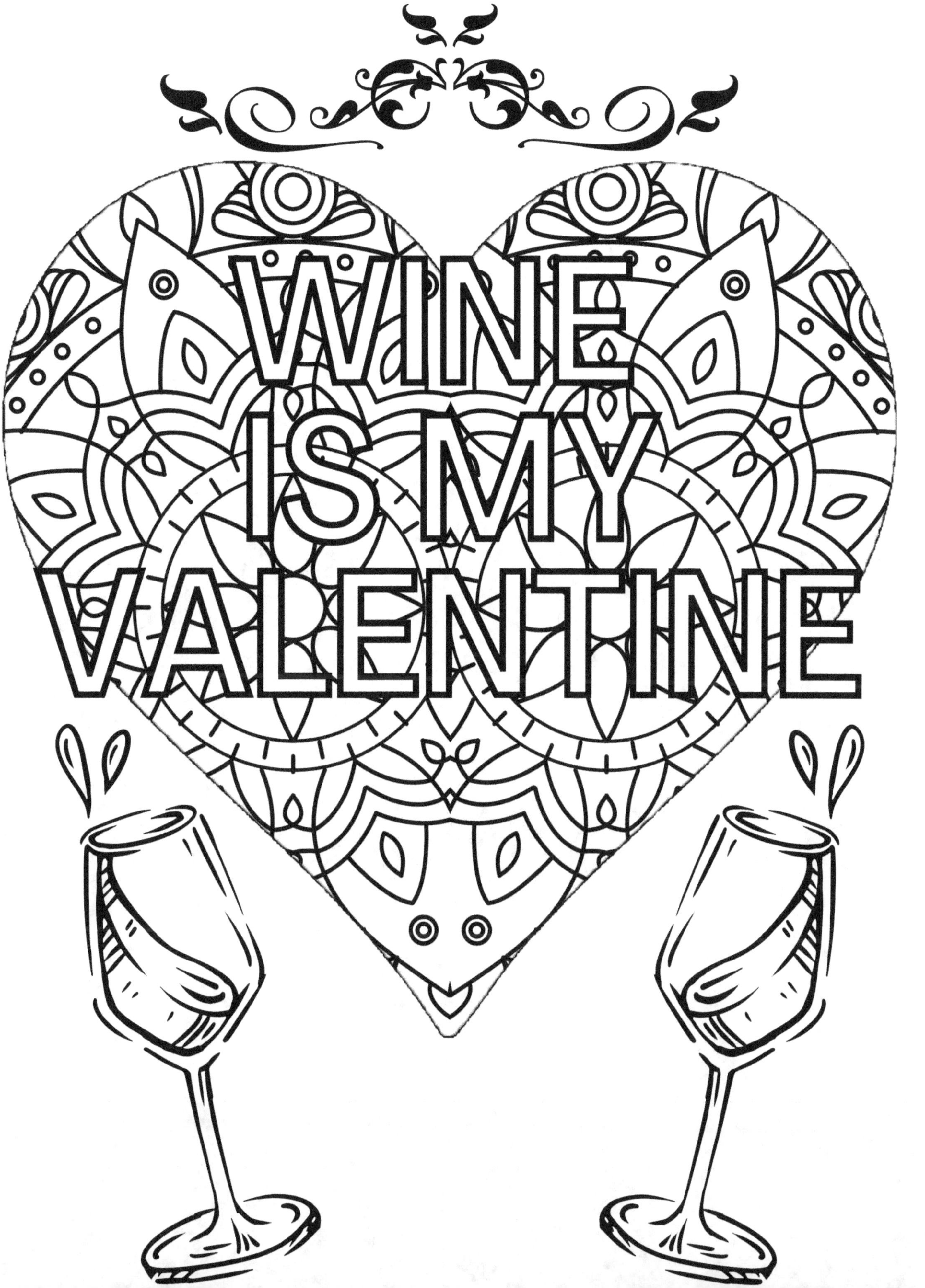
WINE
IS MY
VALENTINE

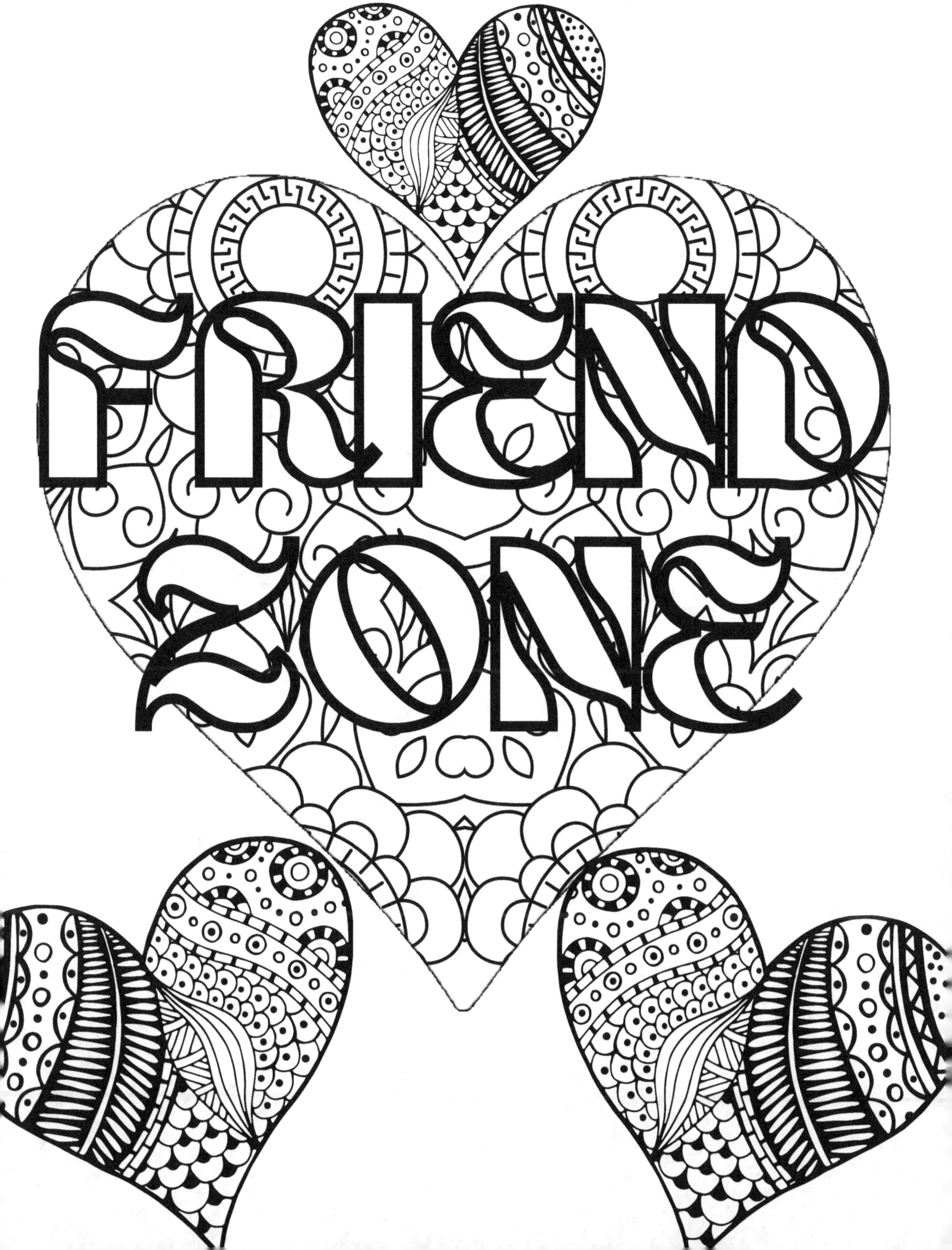
FRIEND
ZONE

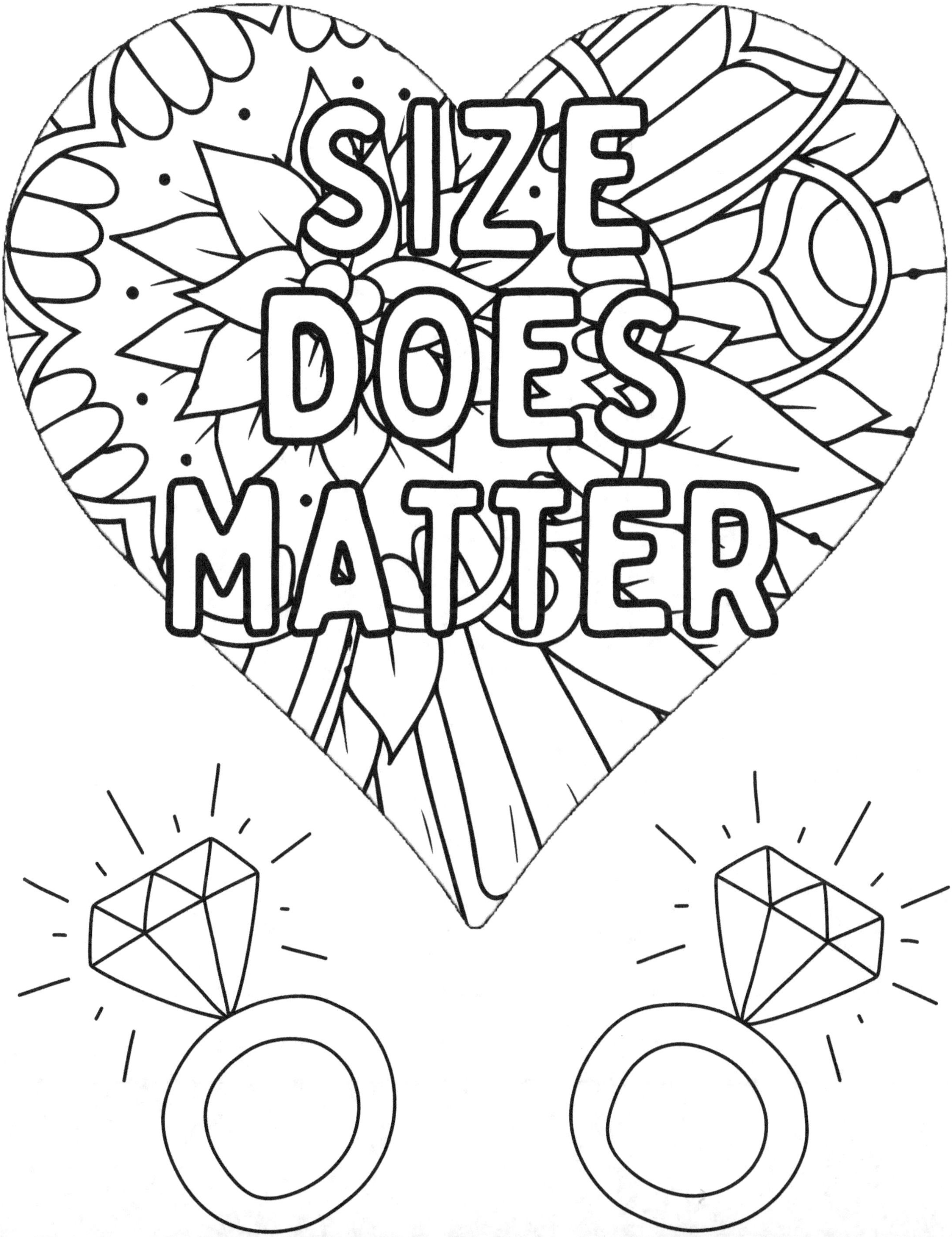
SIZE
DOES
MATTER

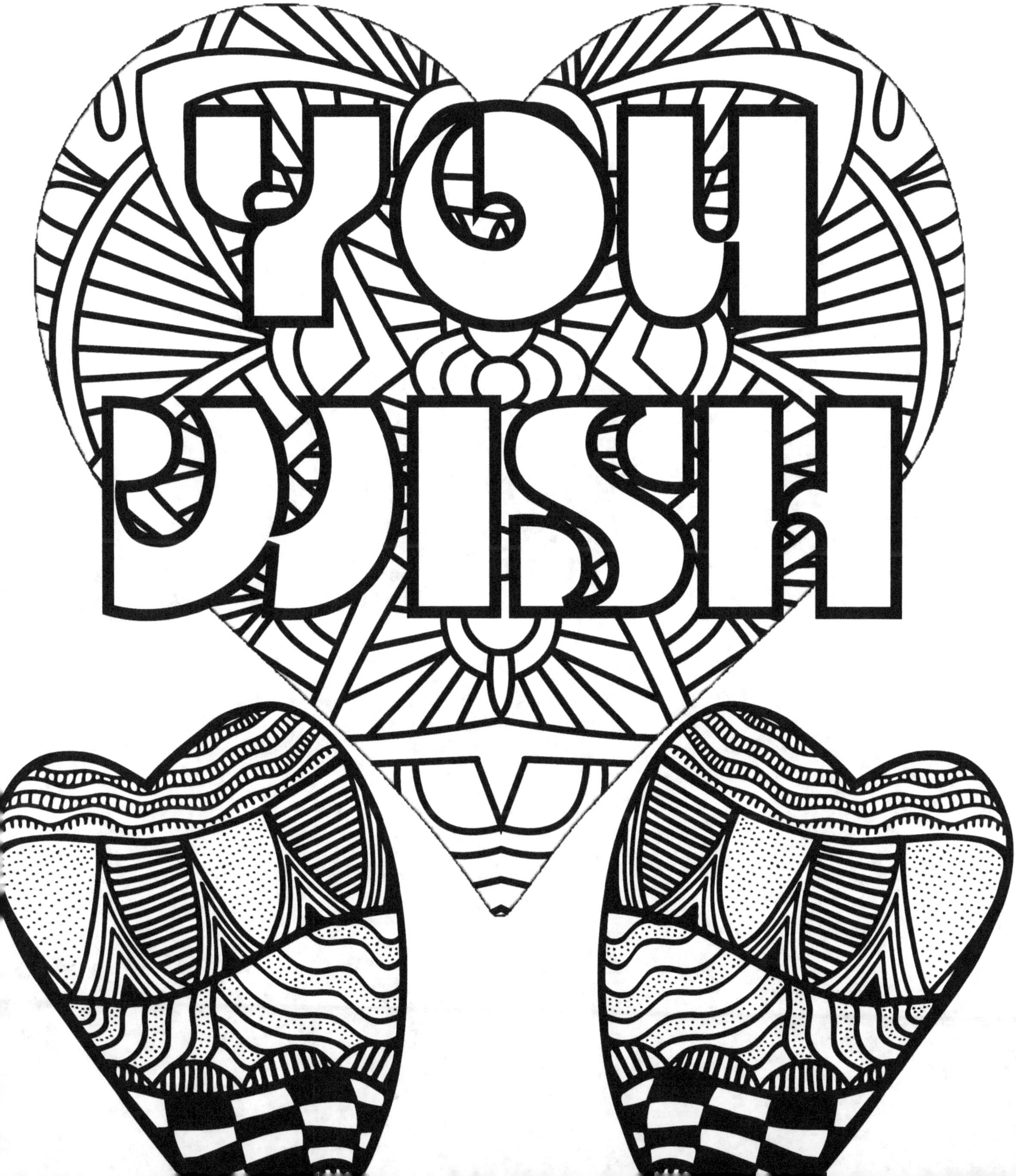
YOU
WISH

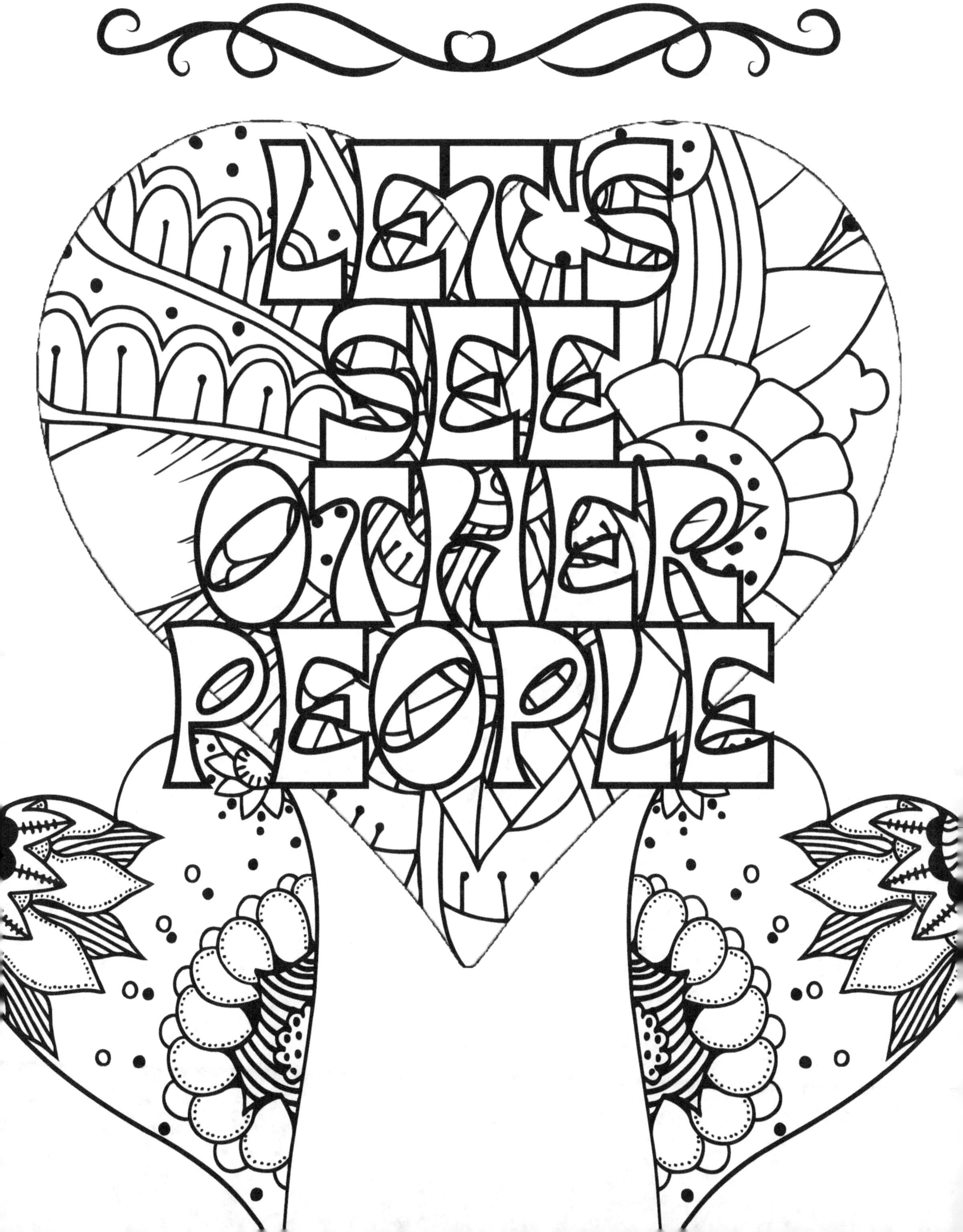
LET'S
SEE
OTHER
PEOPLE

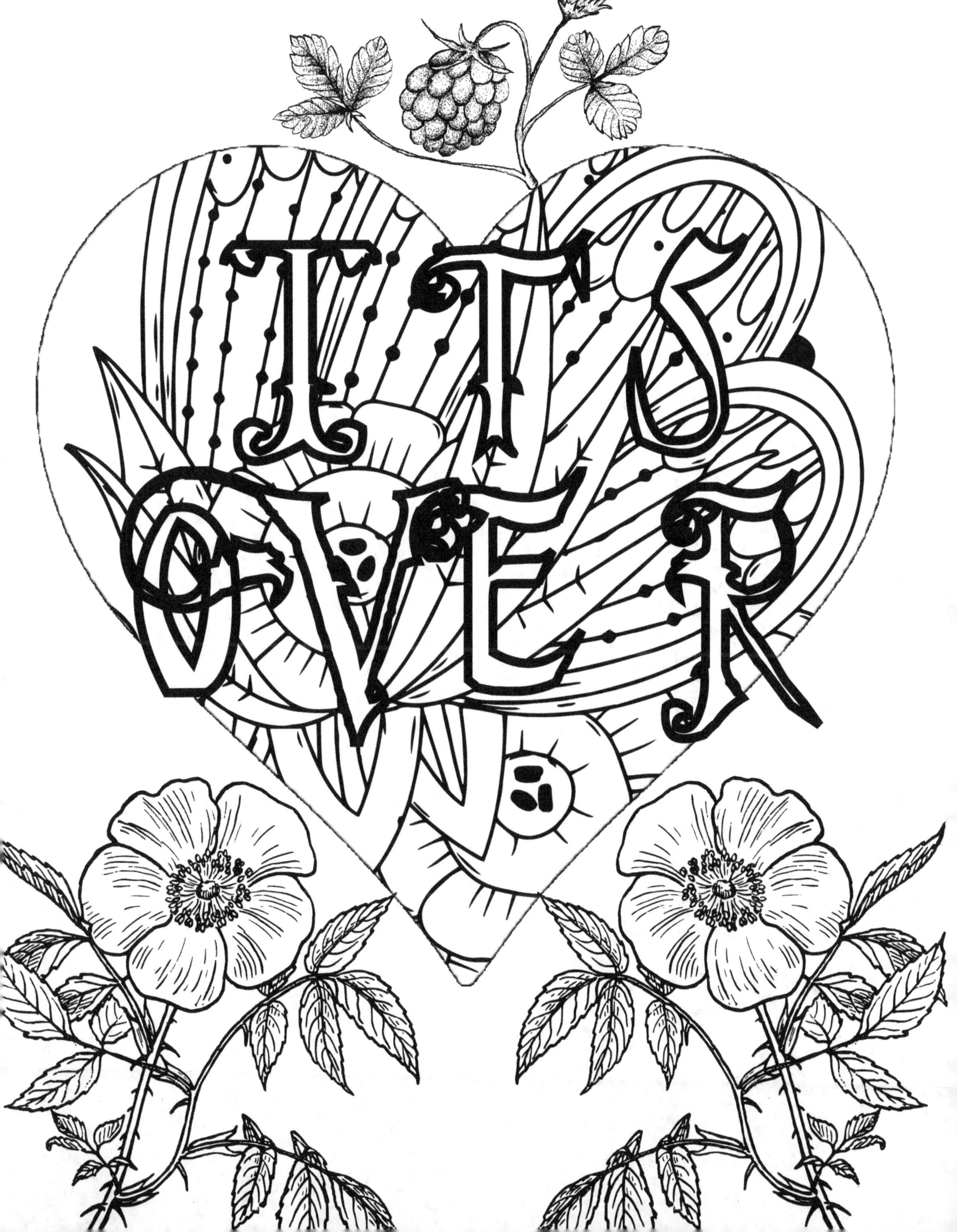
IT'S
OVER

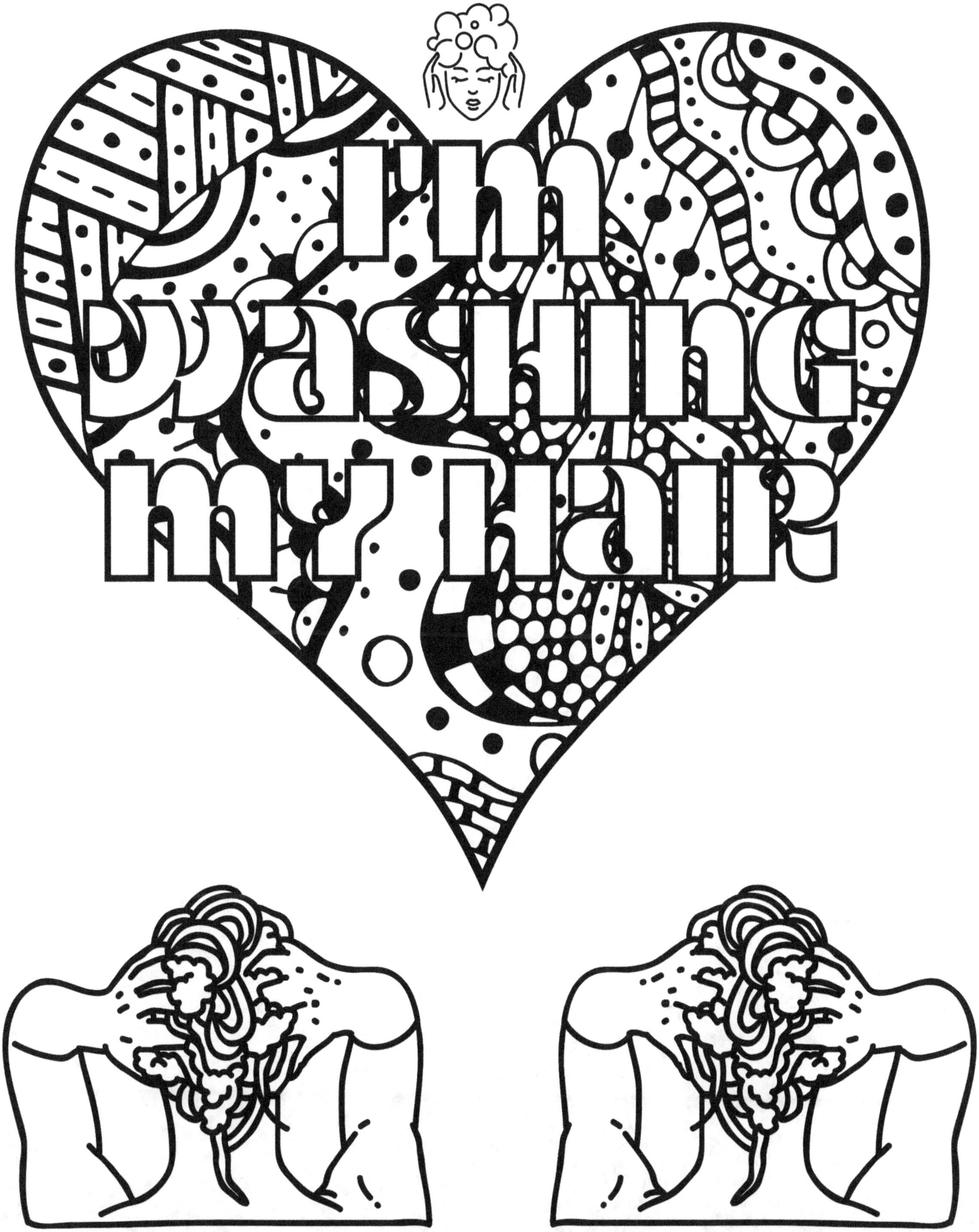
I'M
WASHING
MY HAIR

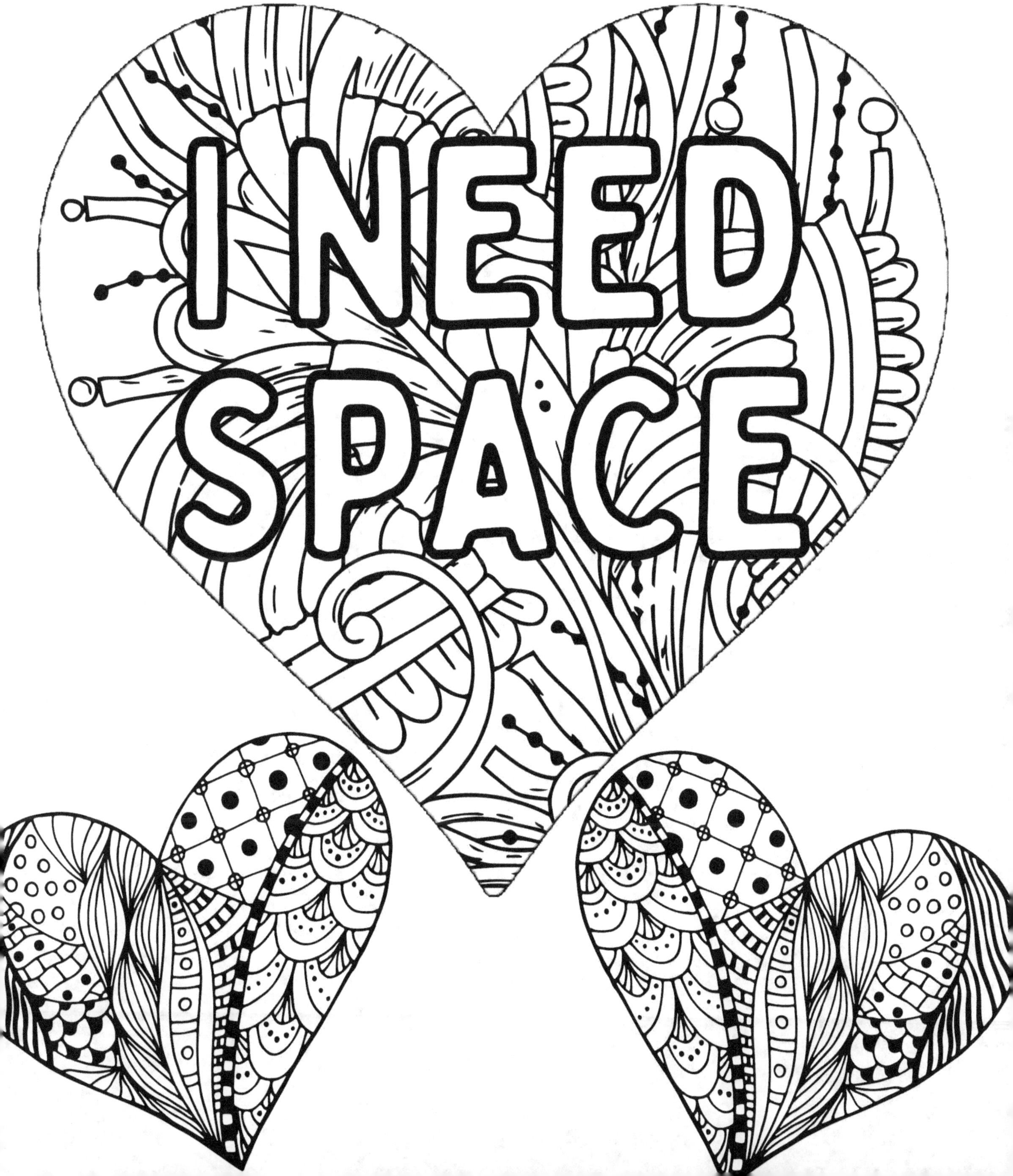
I NEED SPACE

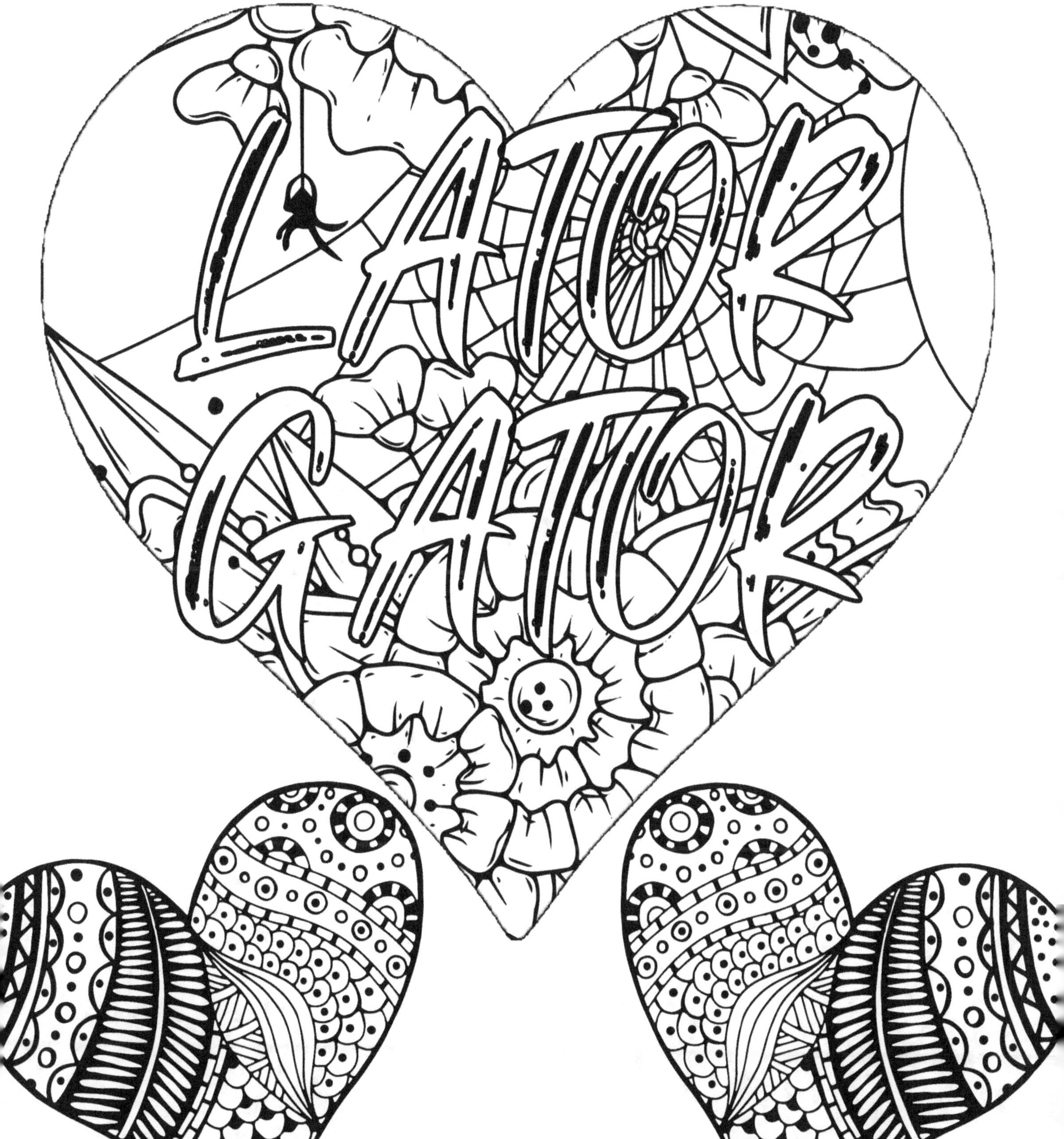
LATOR
GATOR

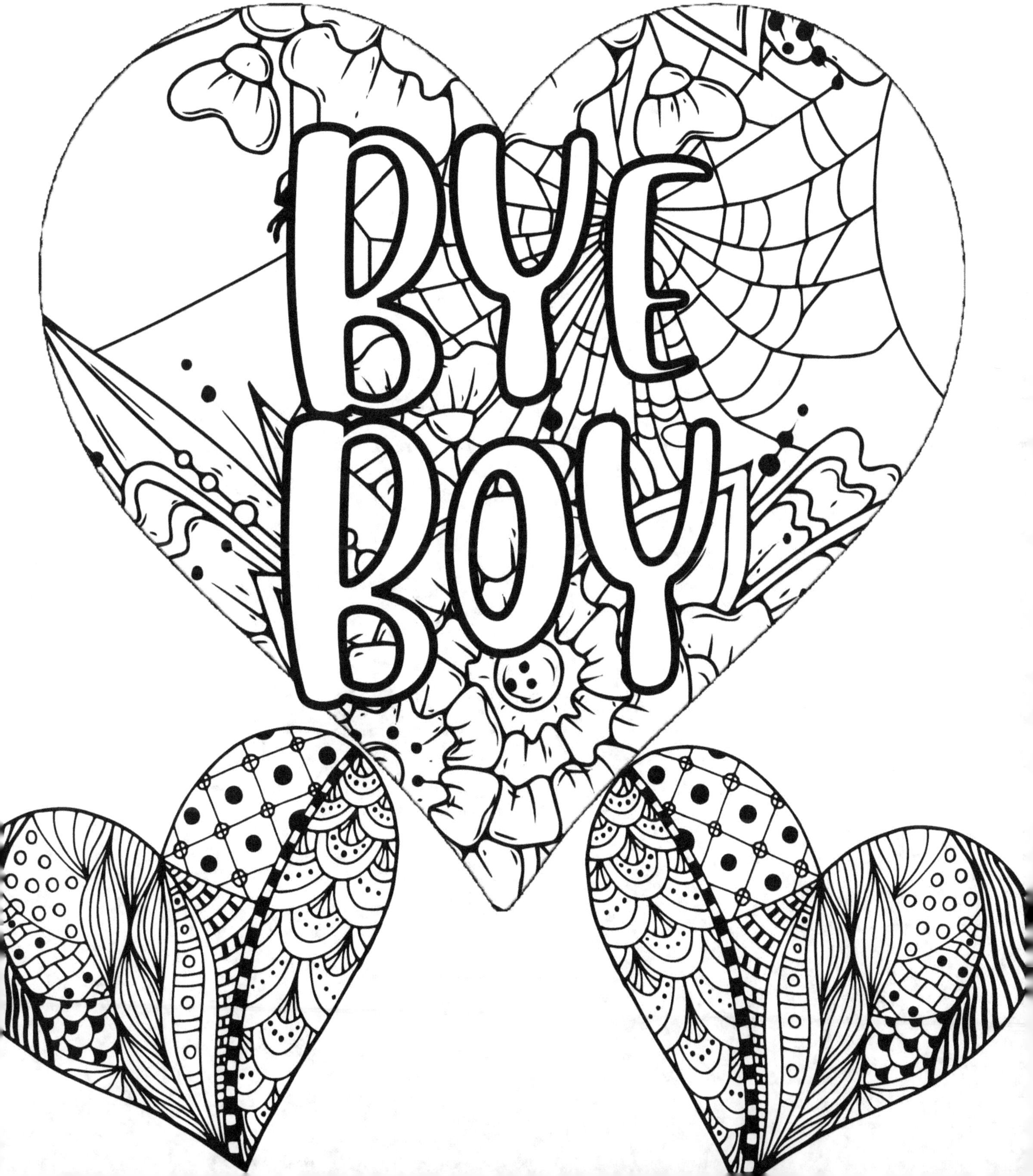
BYE
BOY

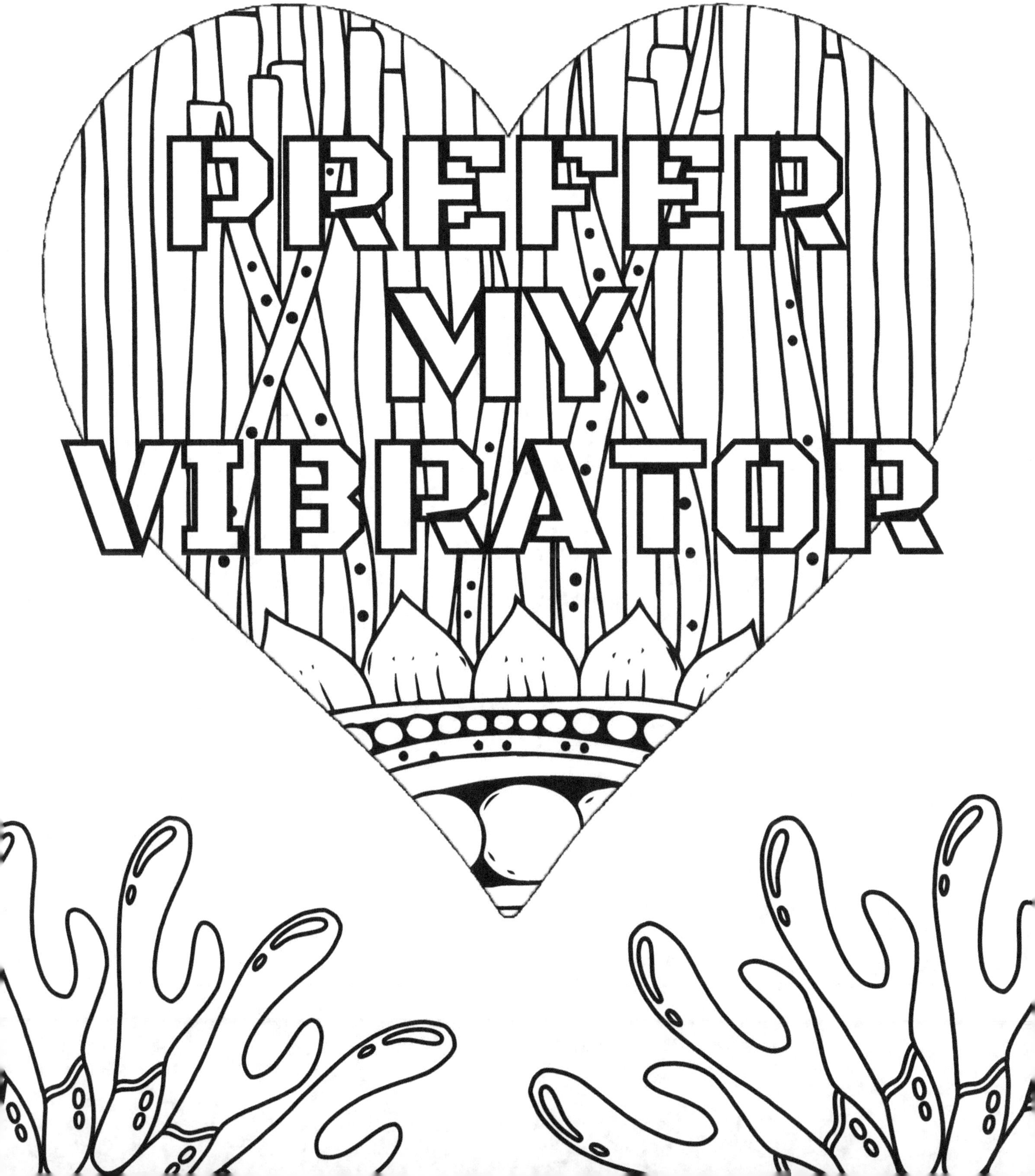
PREFER
MY
VIBRATOR

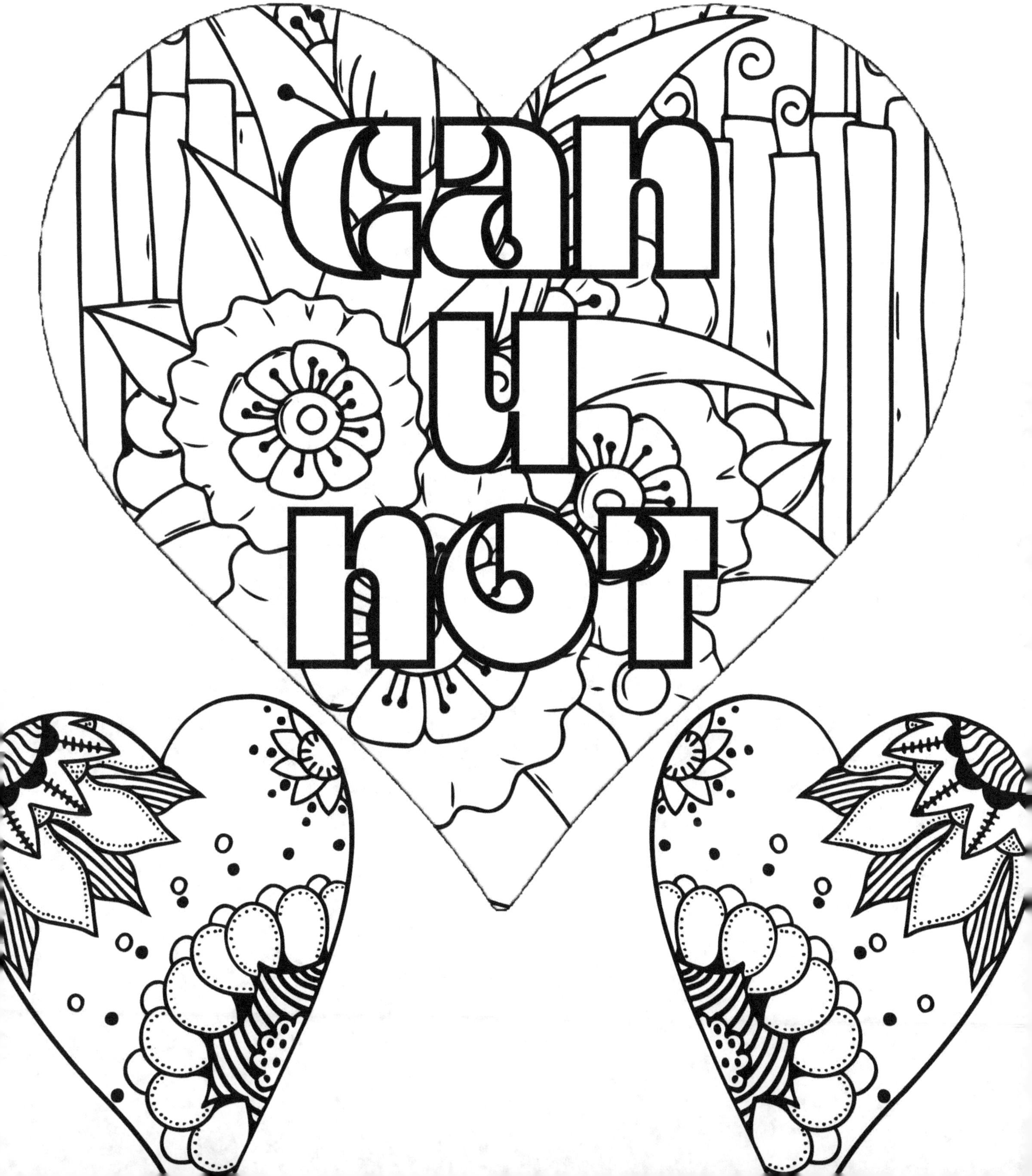
can
u
not

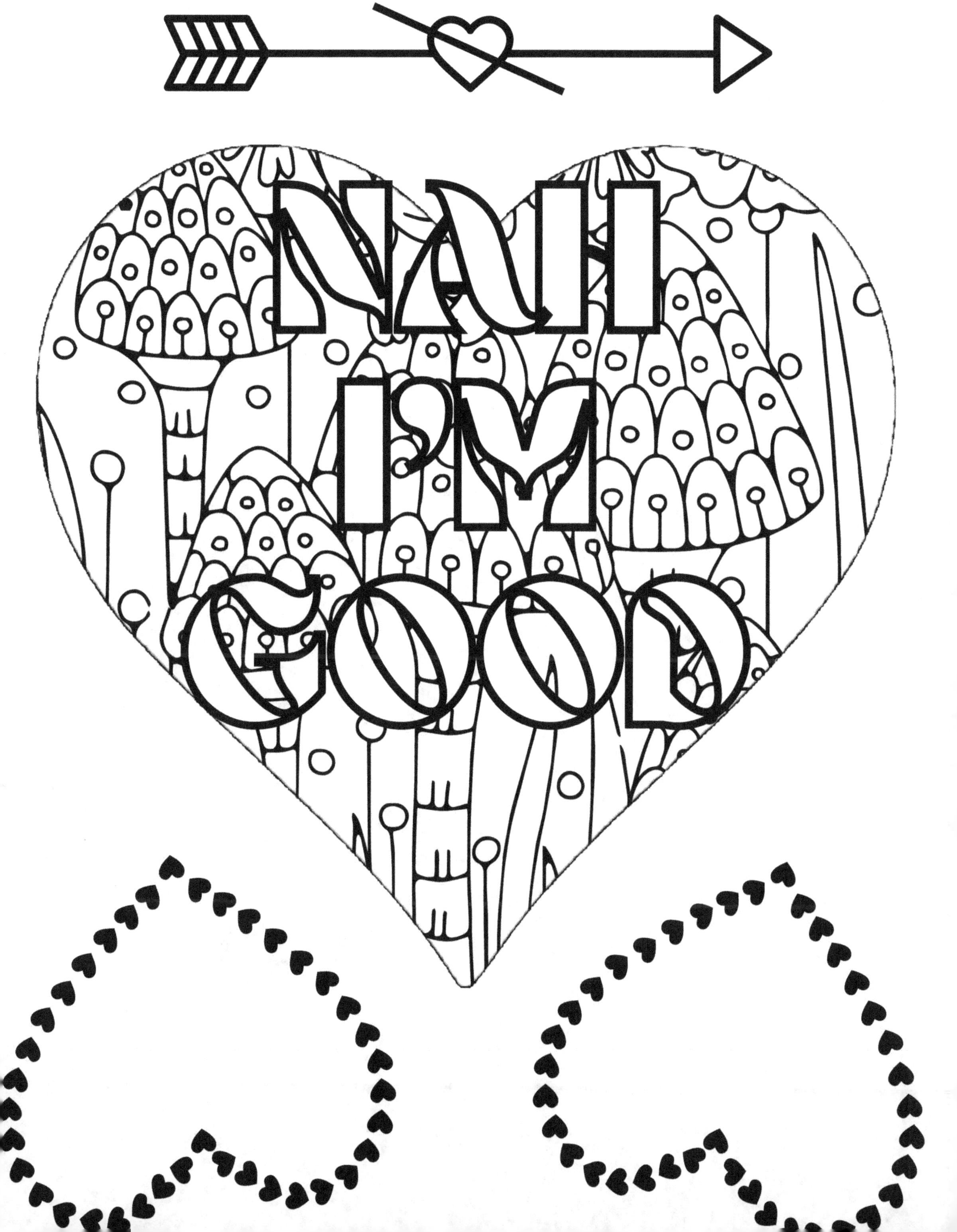
NAH
I'M
GOOD

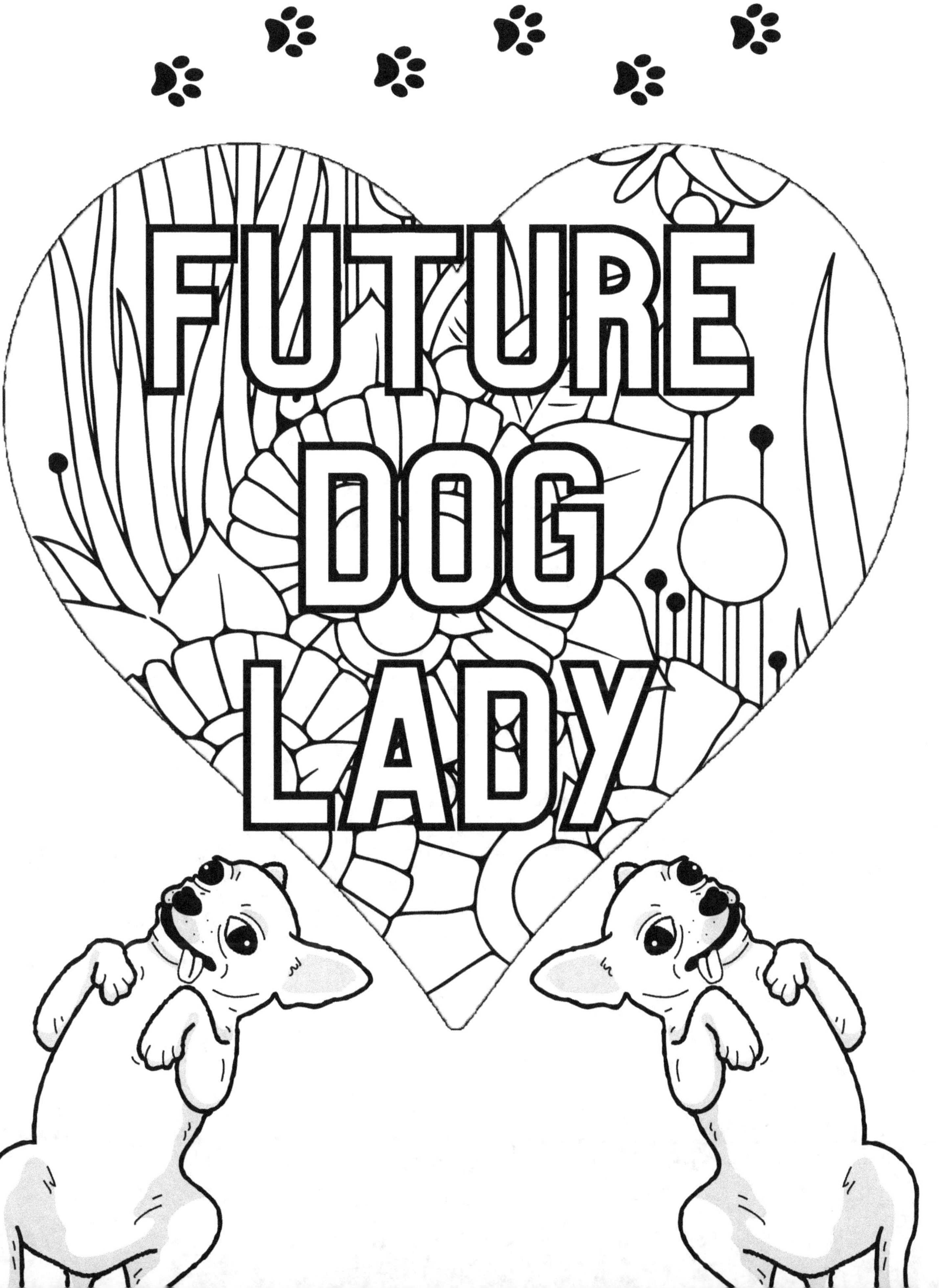
FUTURE
DOG
LADY

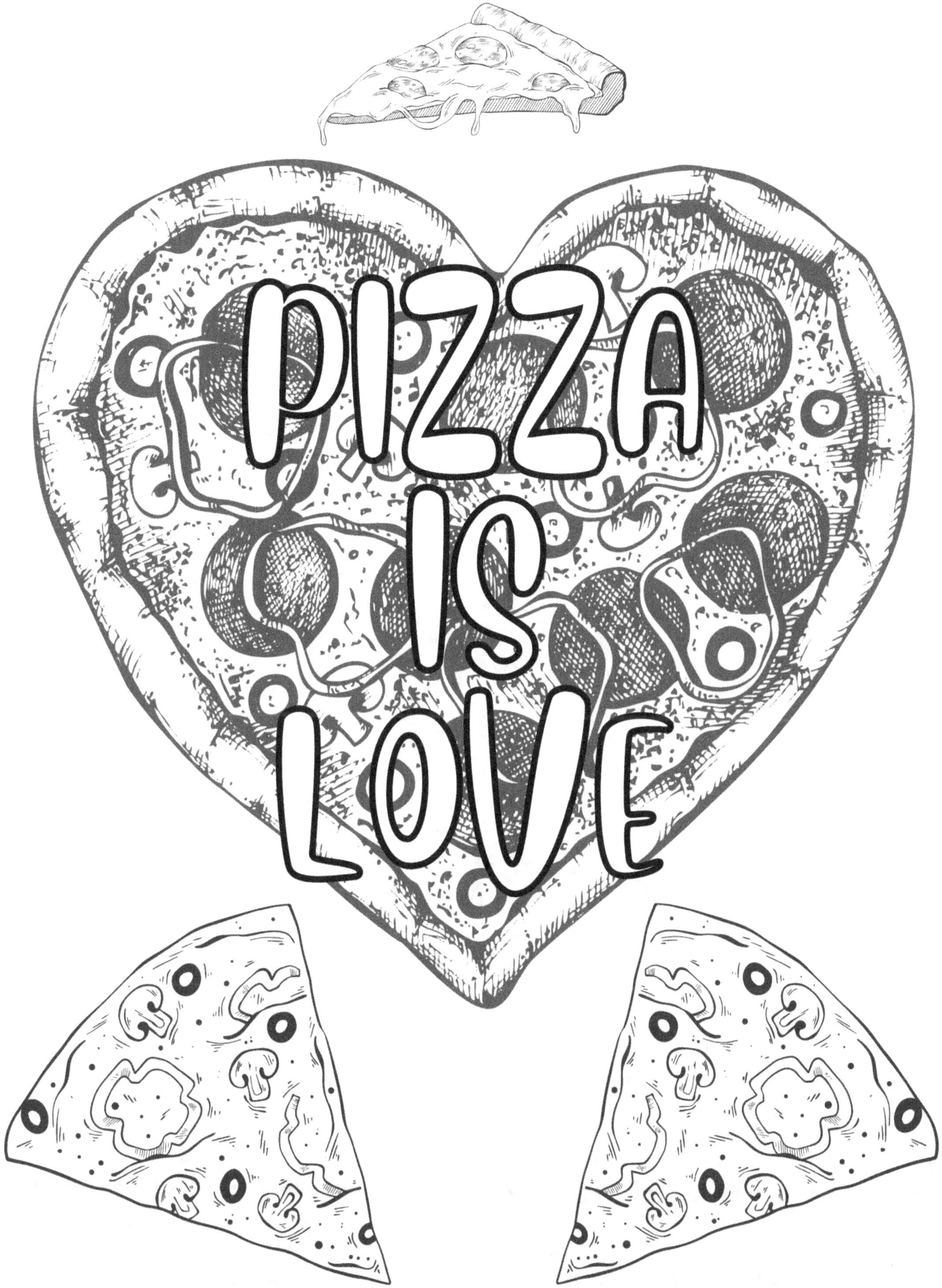
PIZZA
IS
LOVE

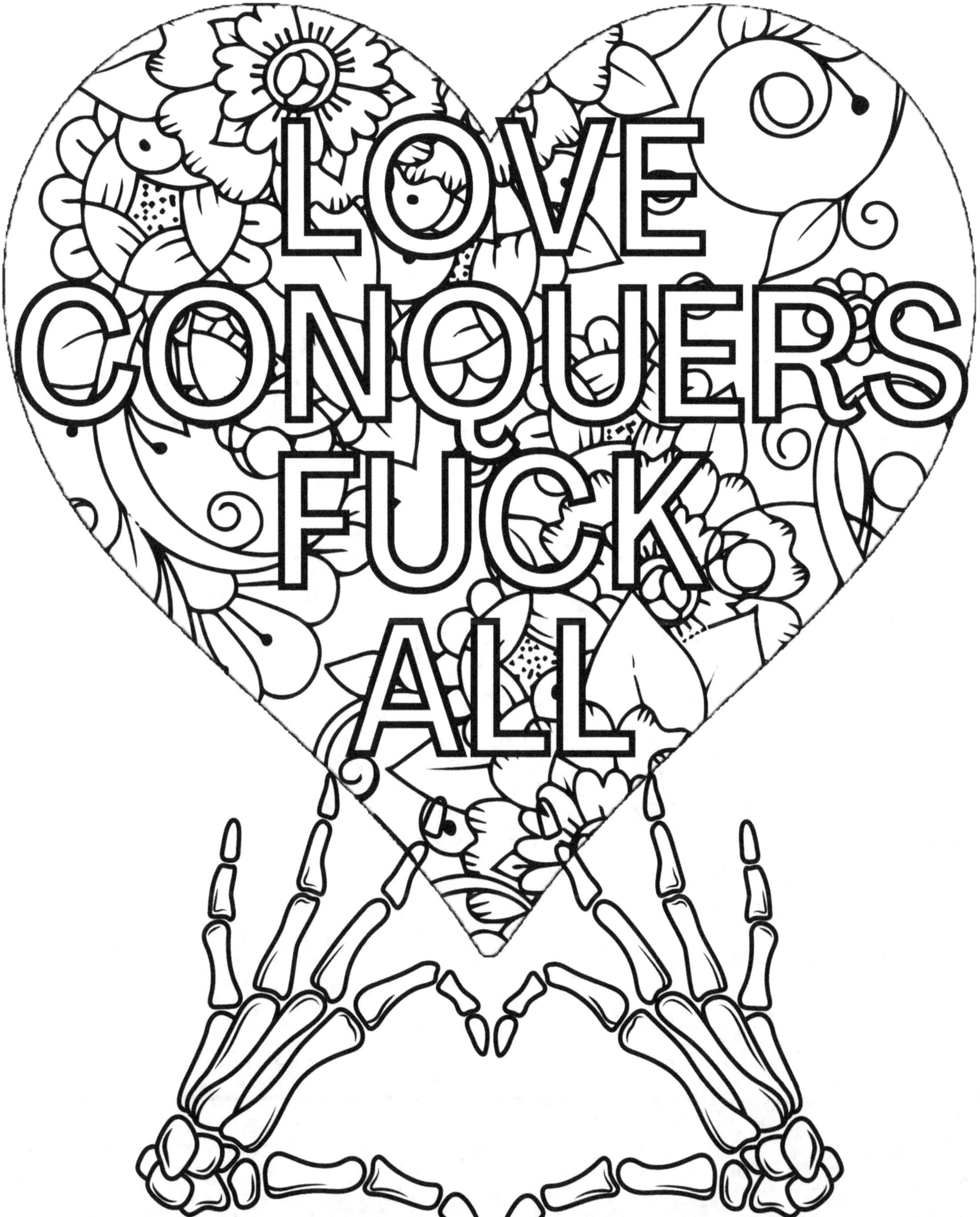
LOVE
CONQUERS
FUCK
ALL

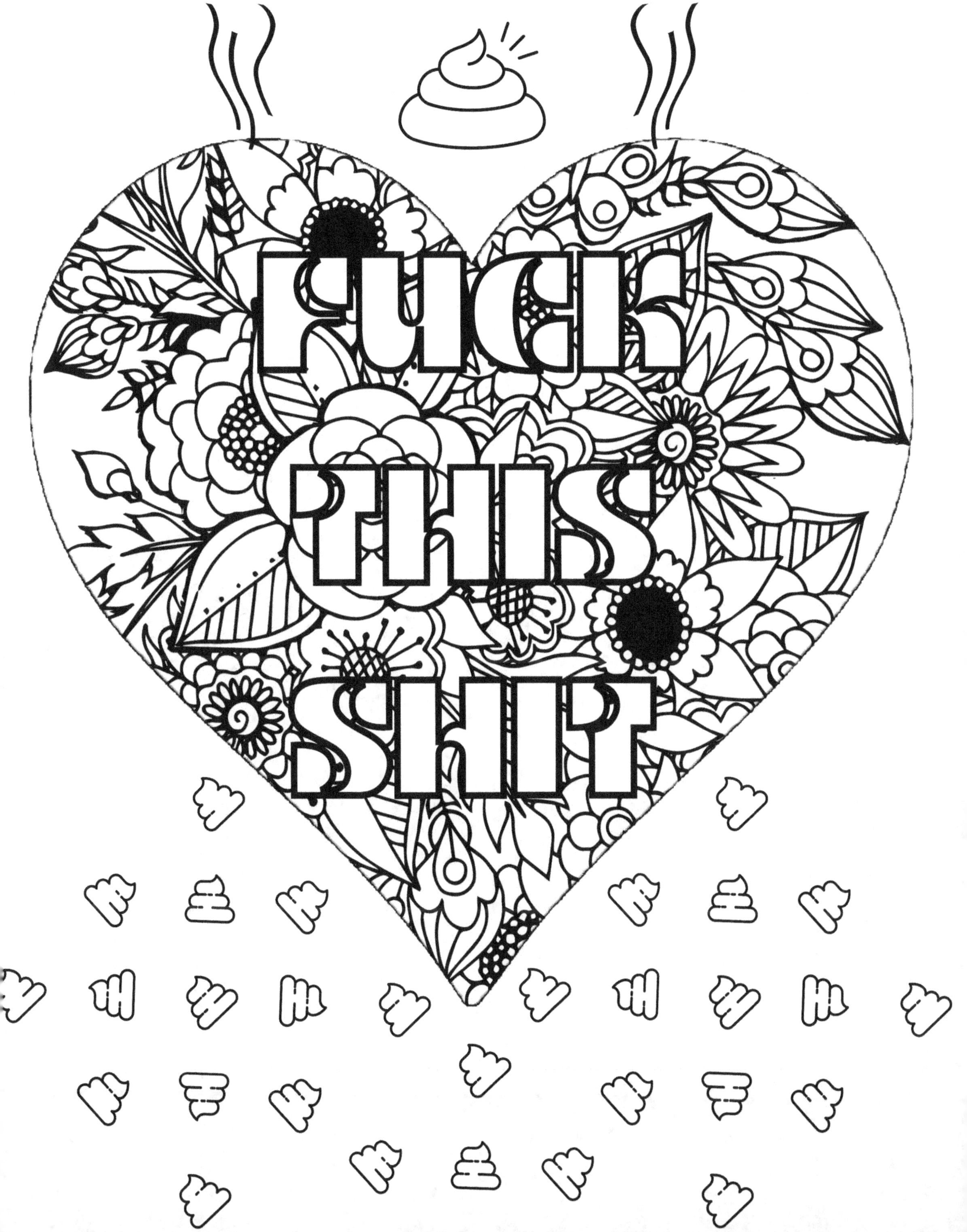
FUCK
THIS
SHIT

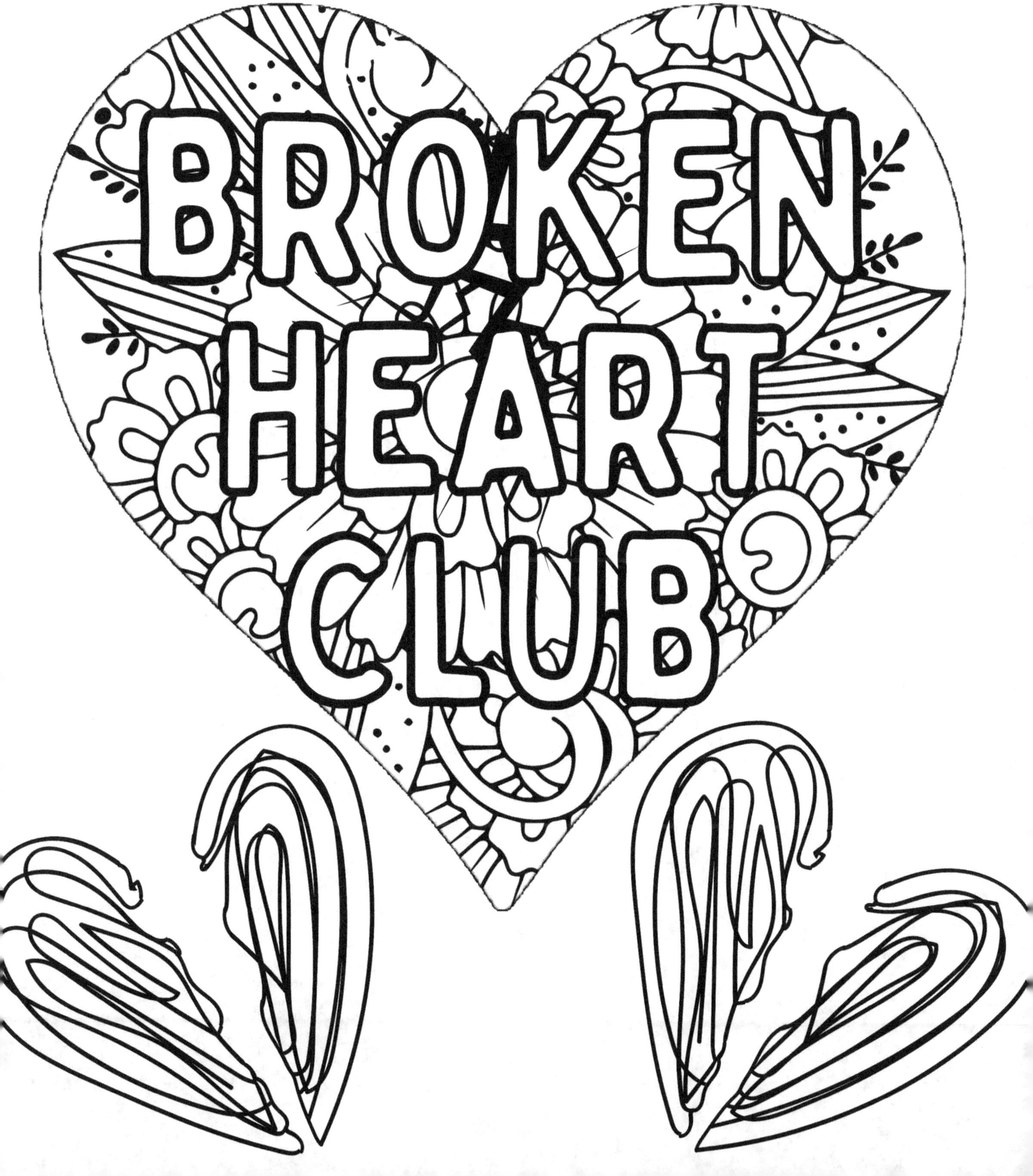
BROKEN
HEART
CLUB

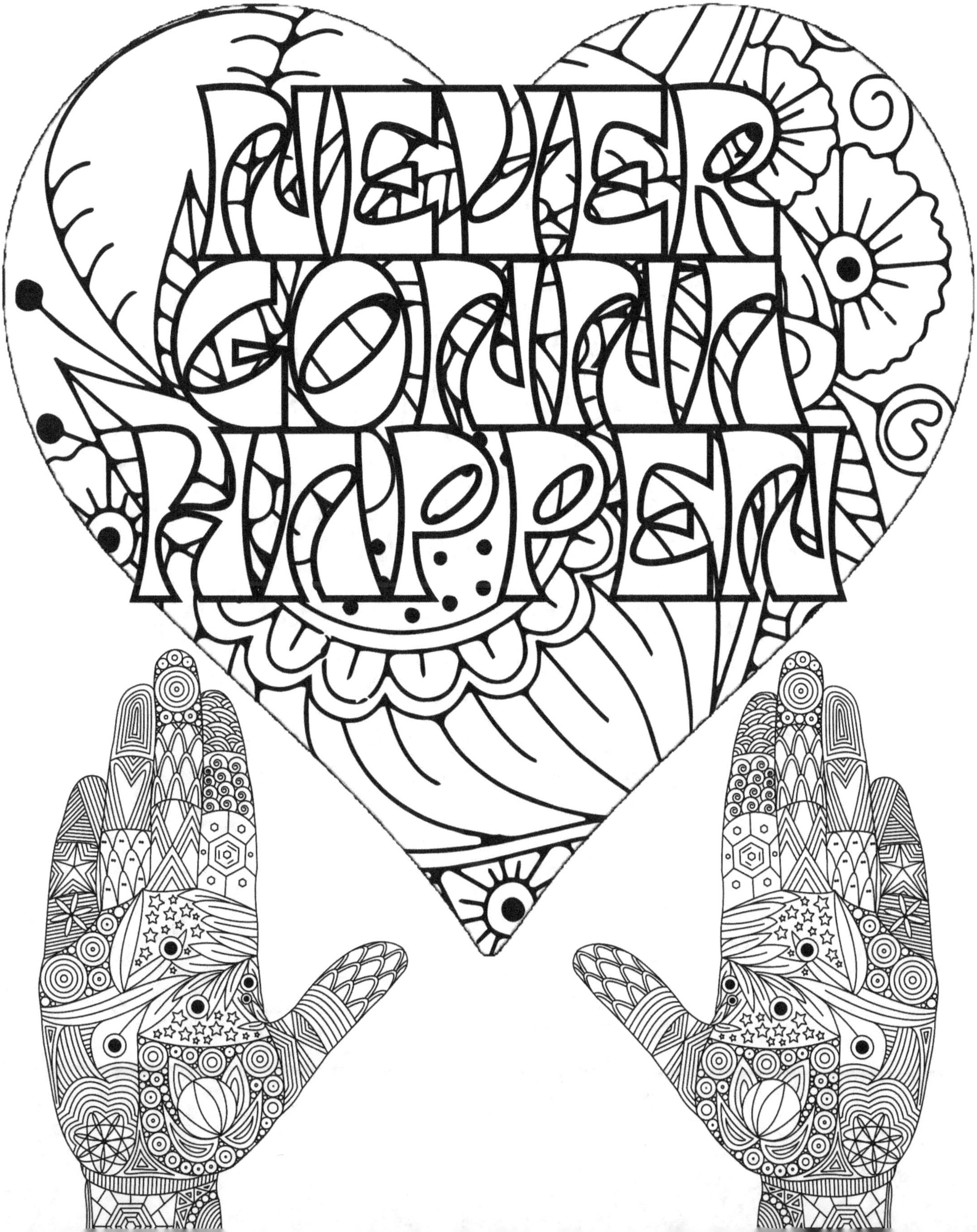
NEVER
GONNA
HAPPEN

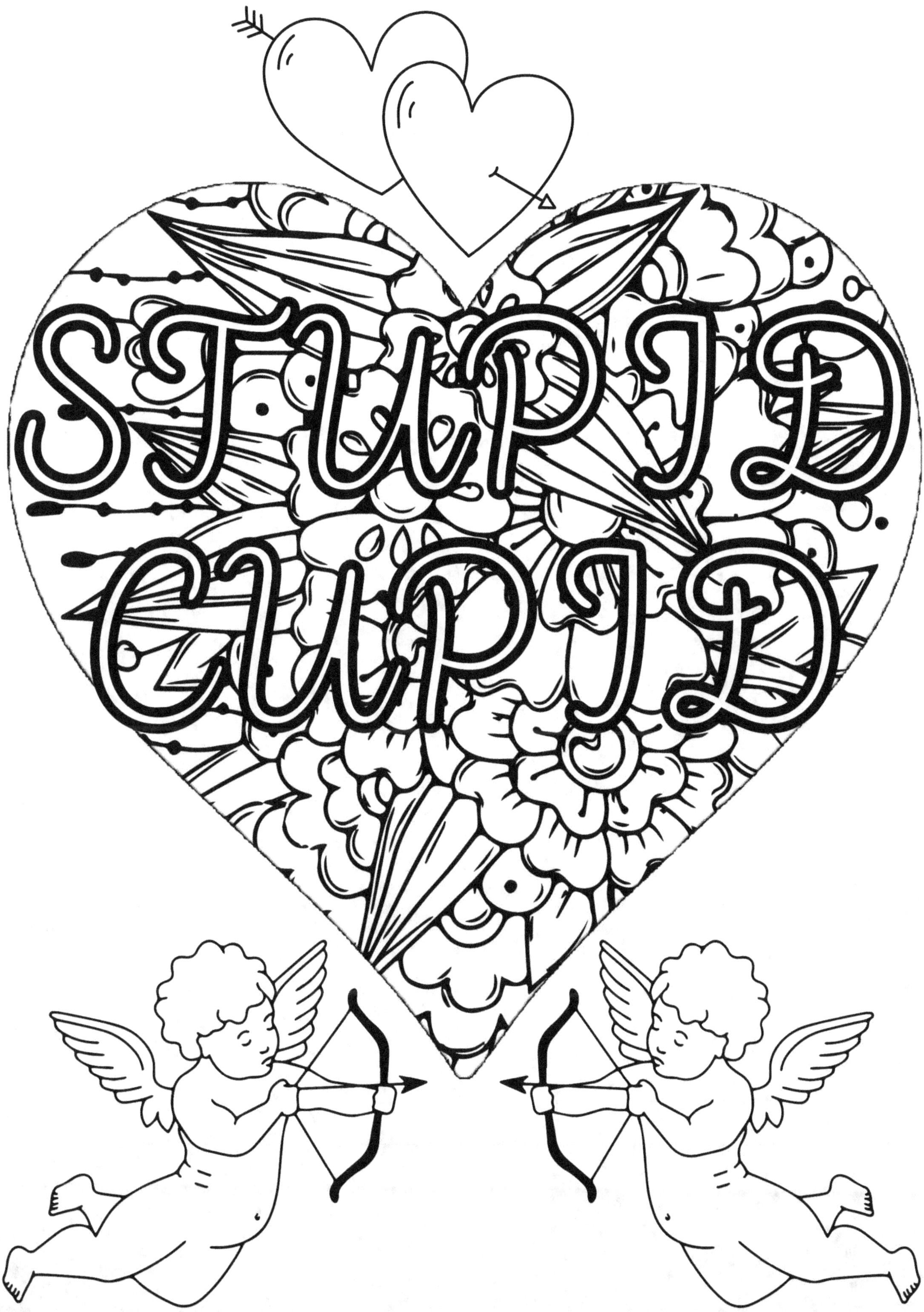
STUPID
CUPID

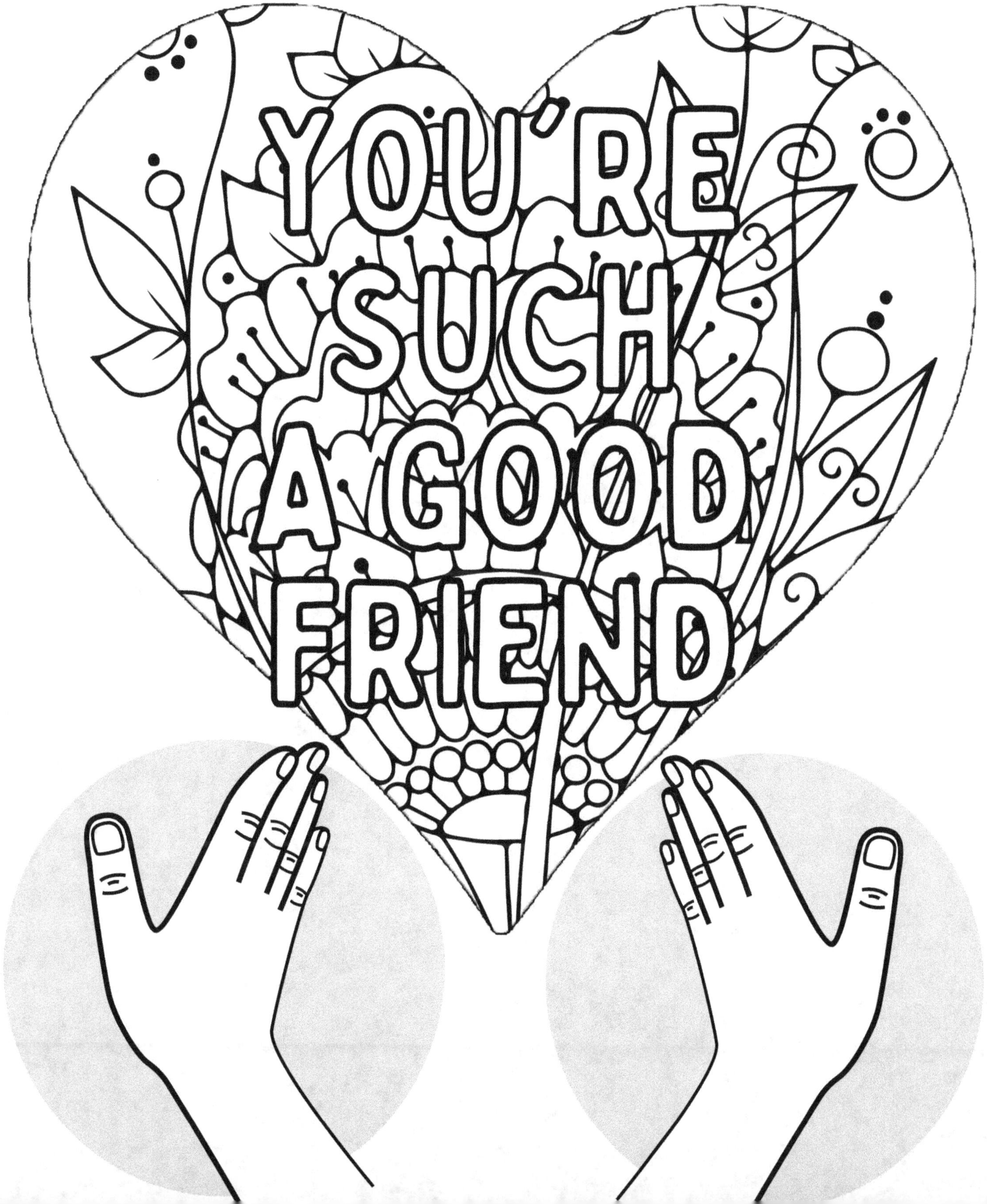
YOU'RE
SUCH
A GOOD
FRIEND

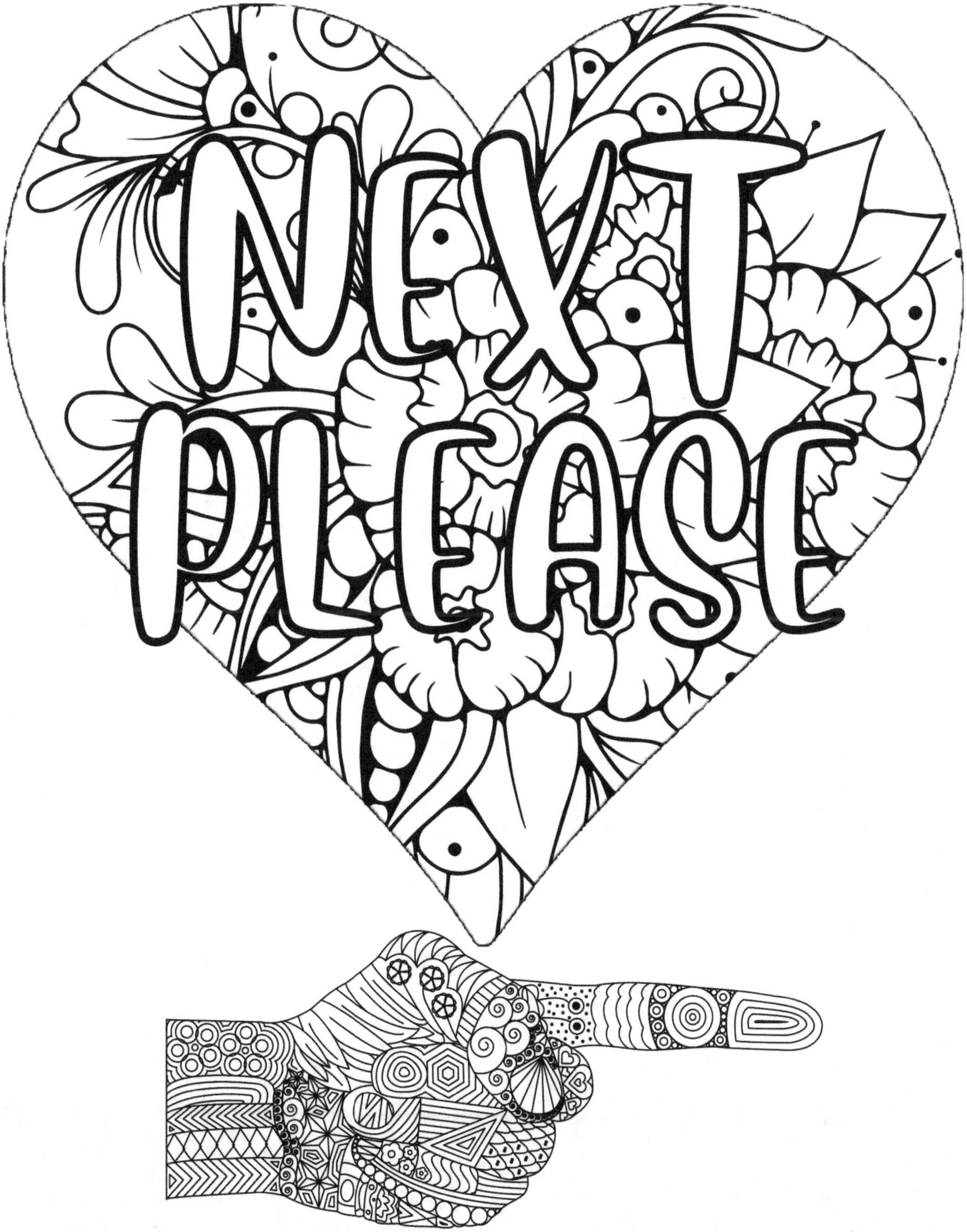
NEXT
PLEASE

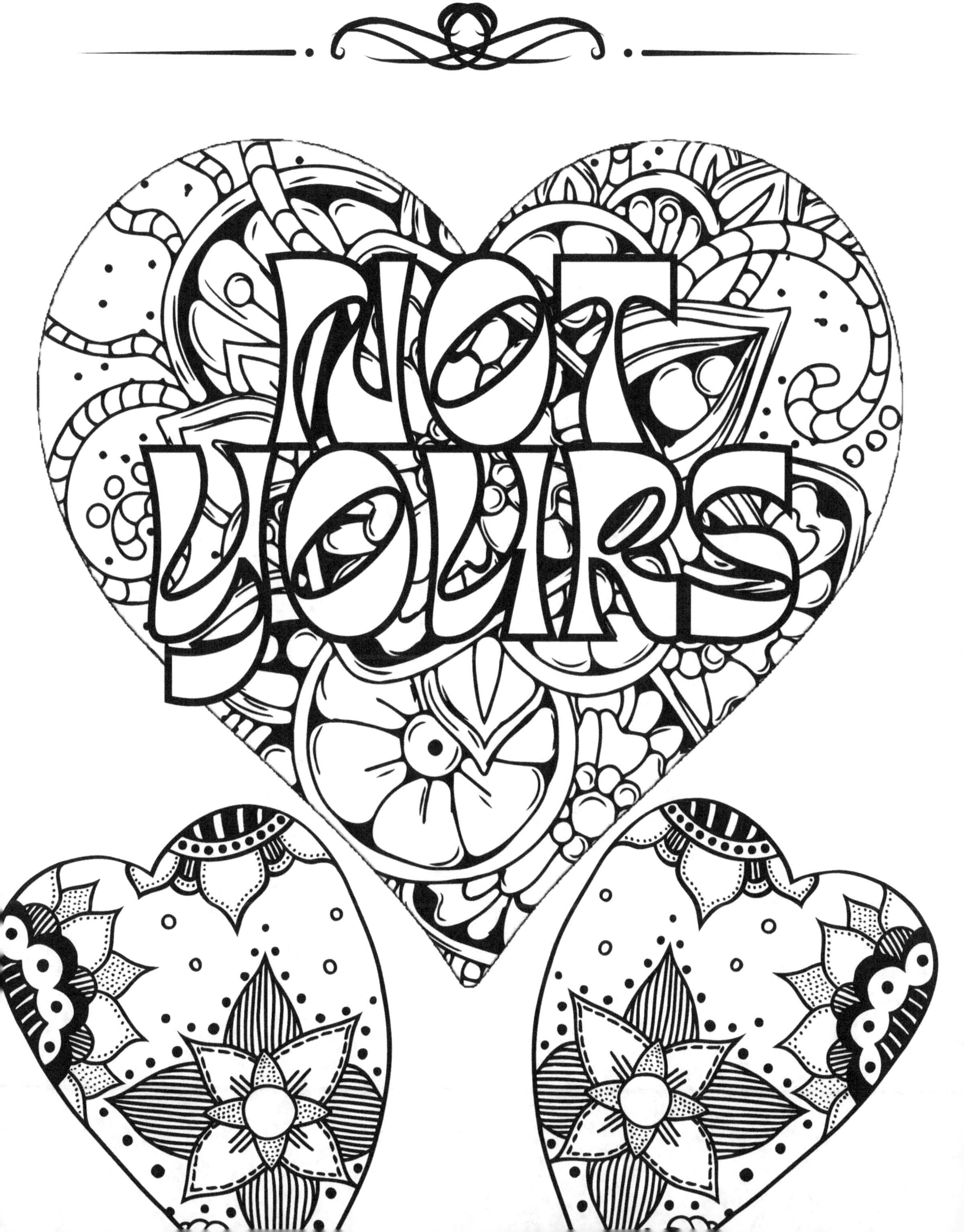
NOT
YOURS

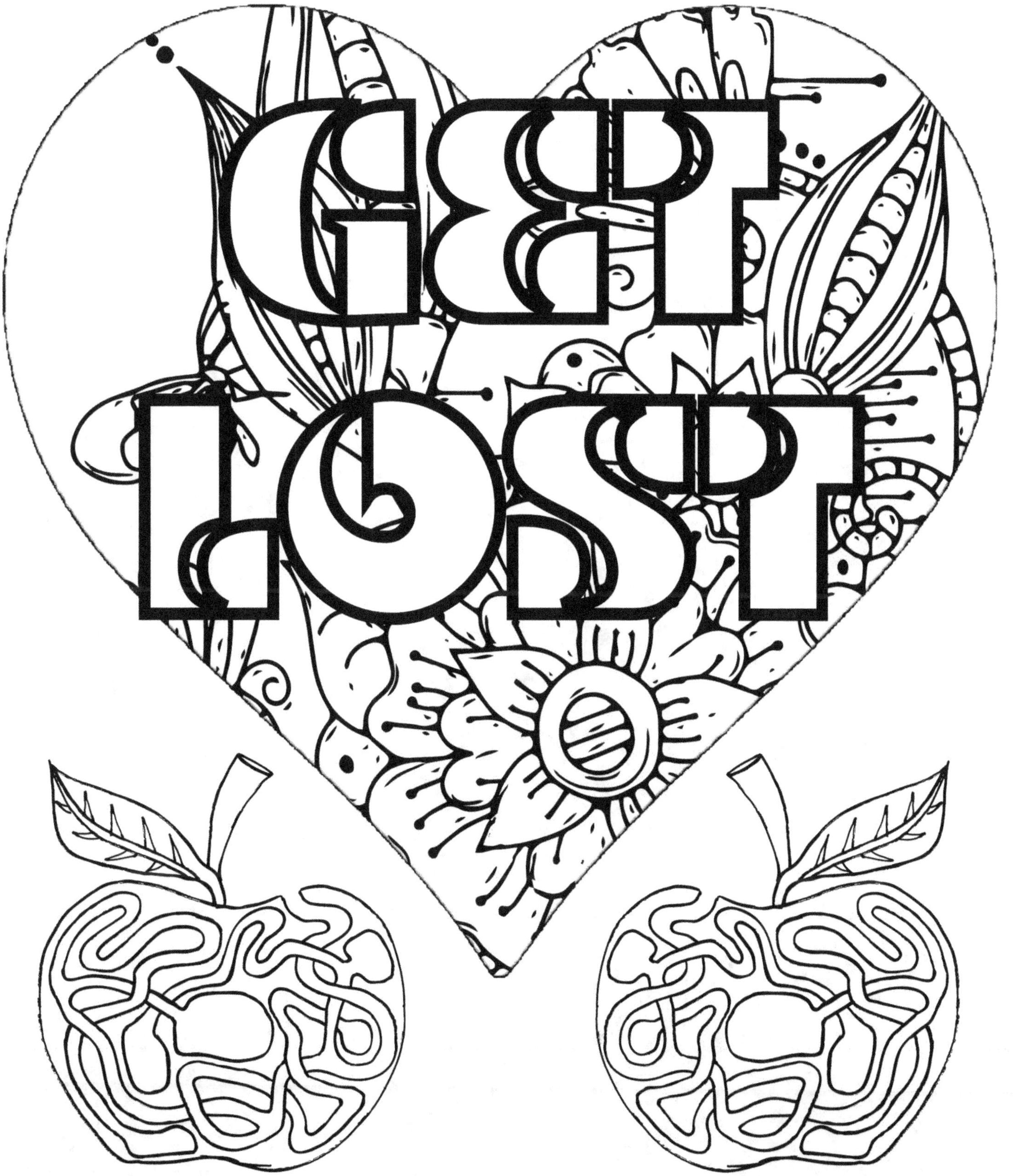
GET
LOST

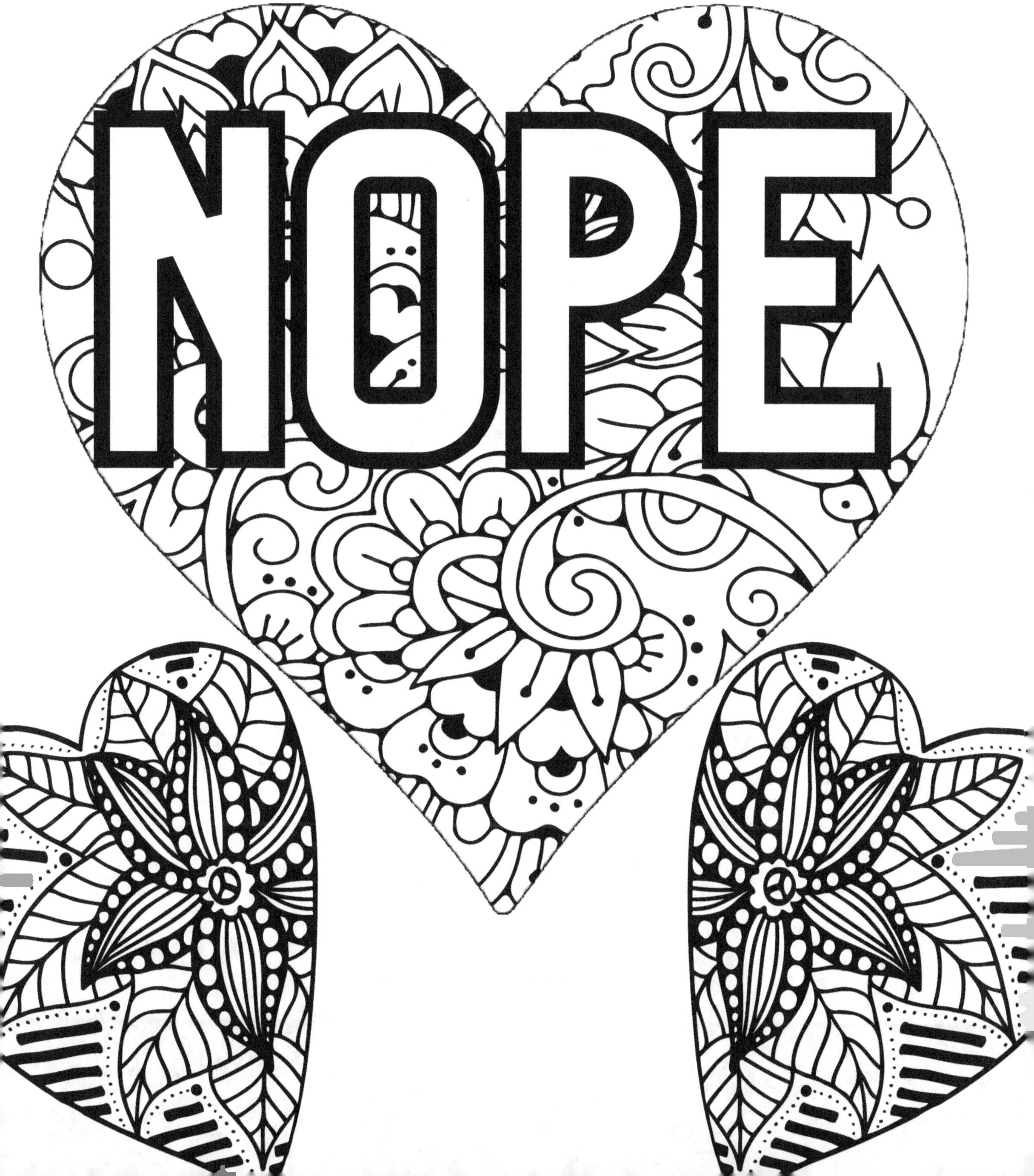
NOPE

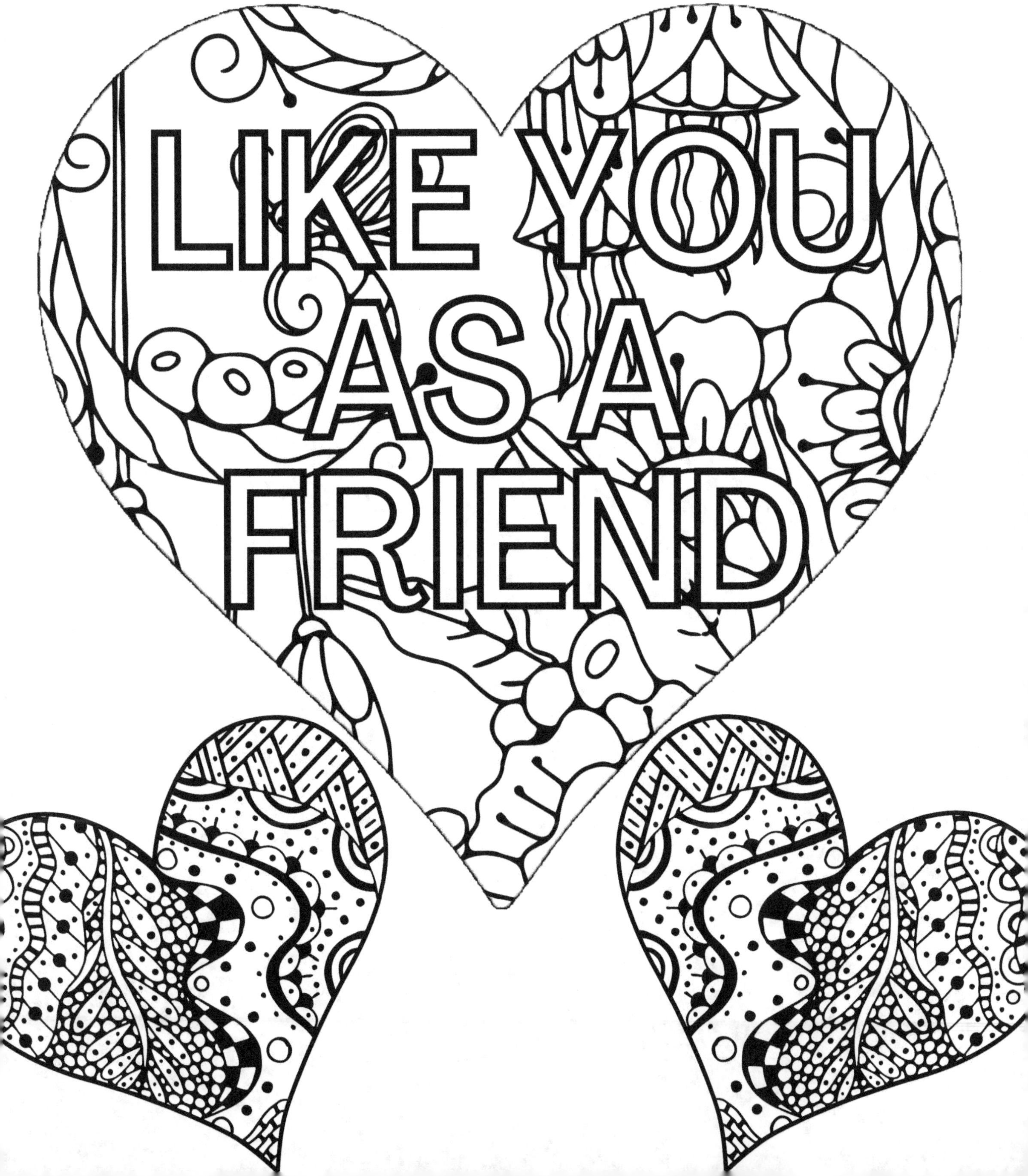
LIKE YOU
AS A
FRIEND

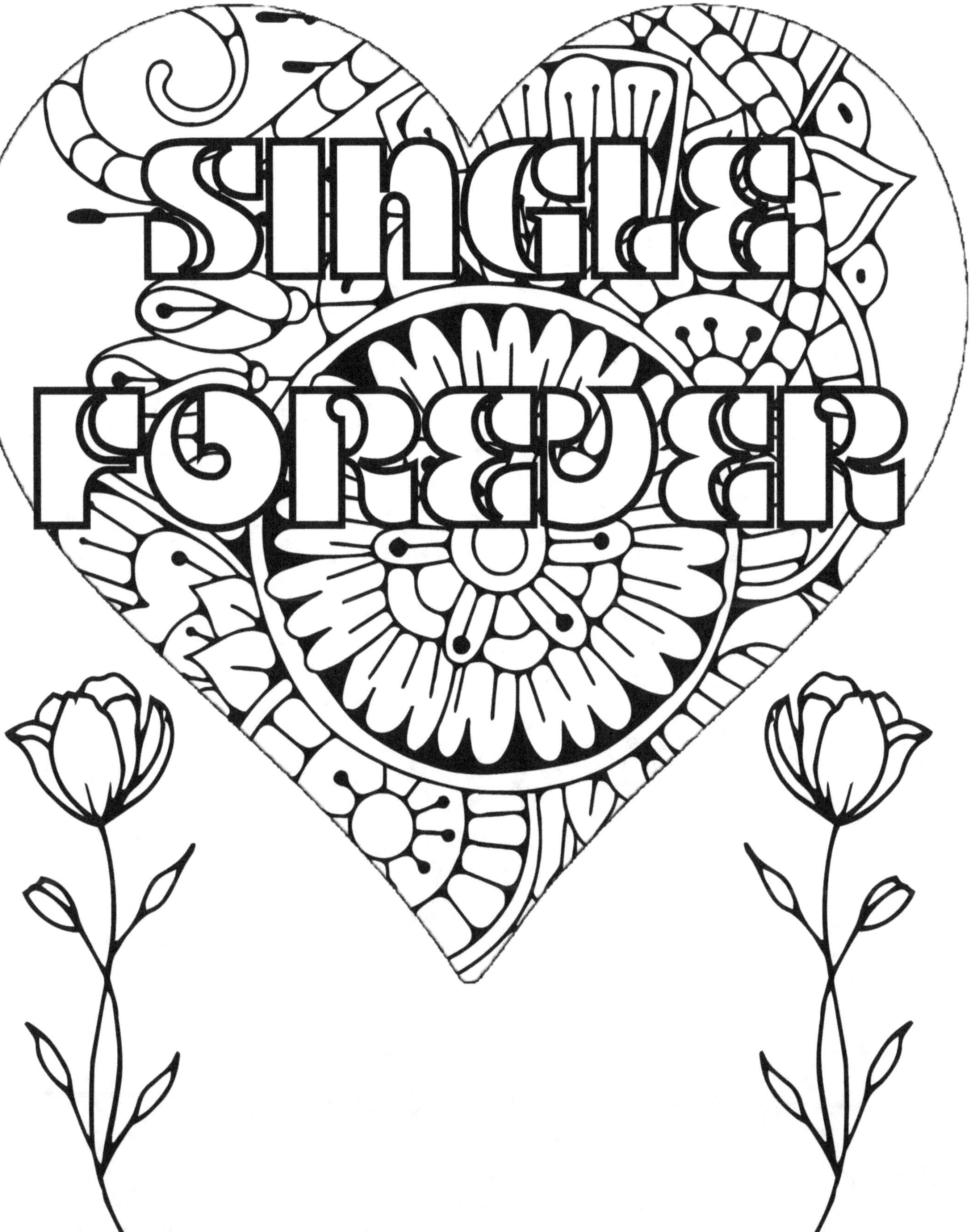
SINGLE
FOREVER

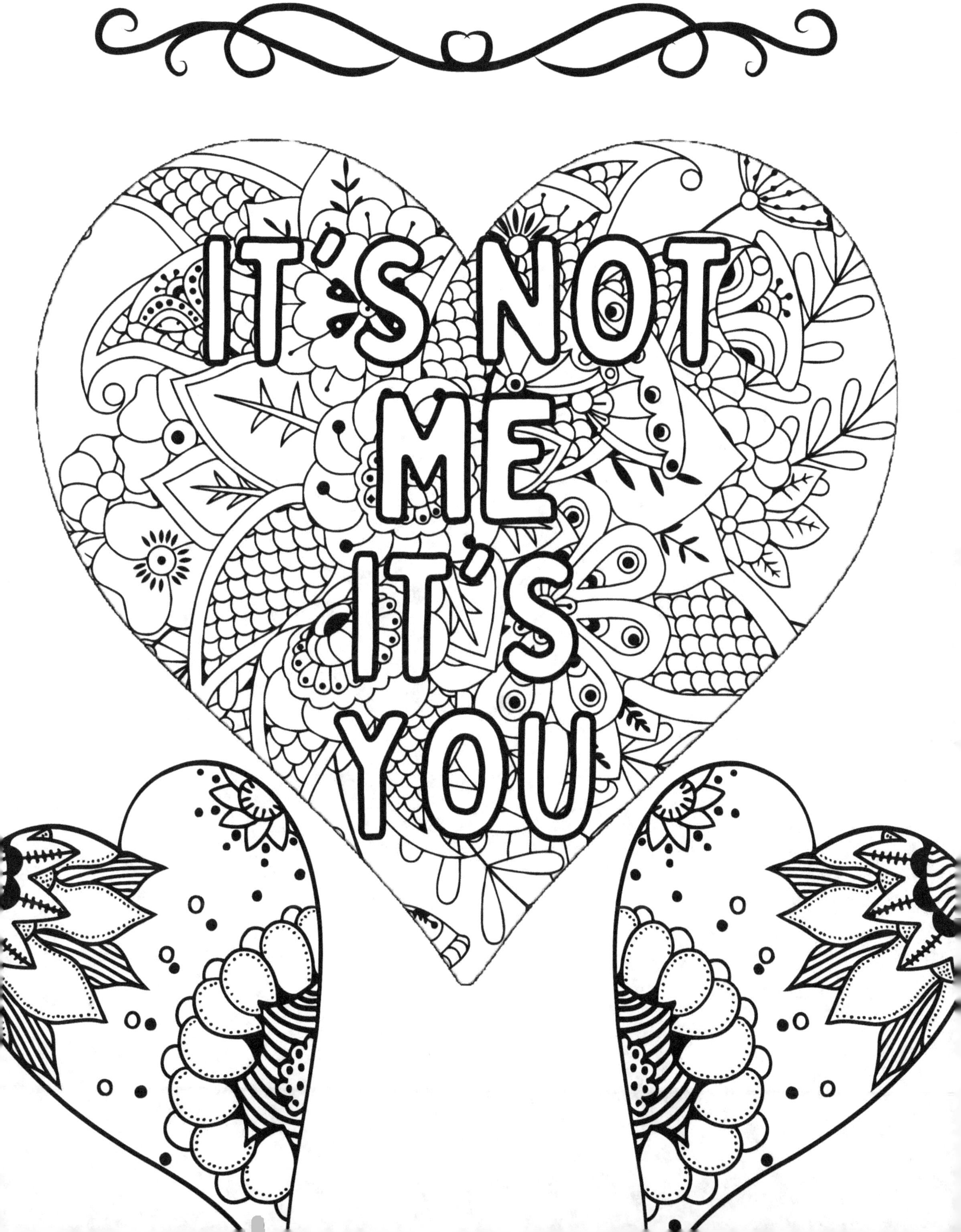
IT'S NOT
ME
IT'S
YOU

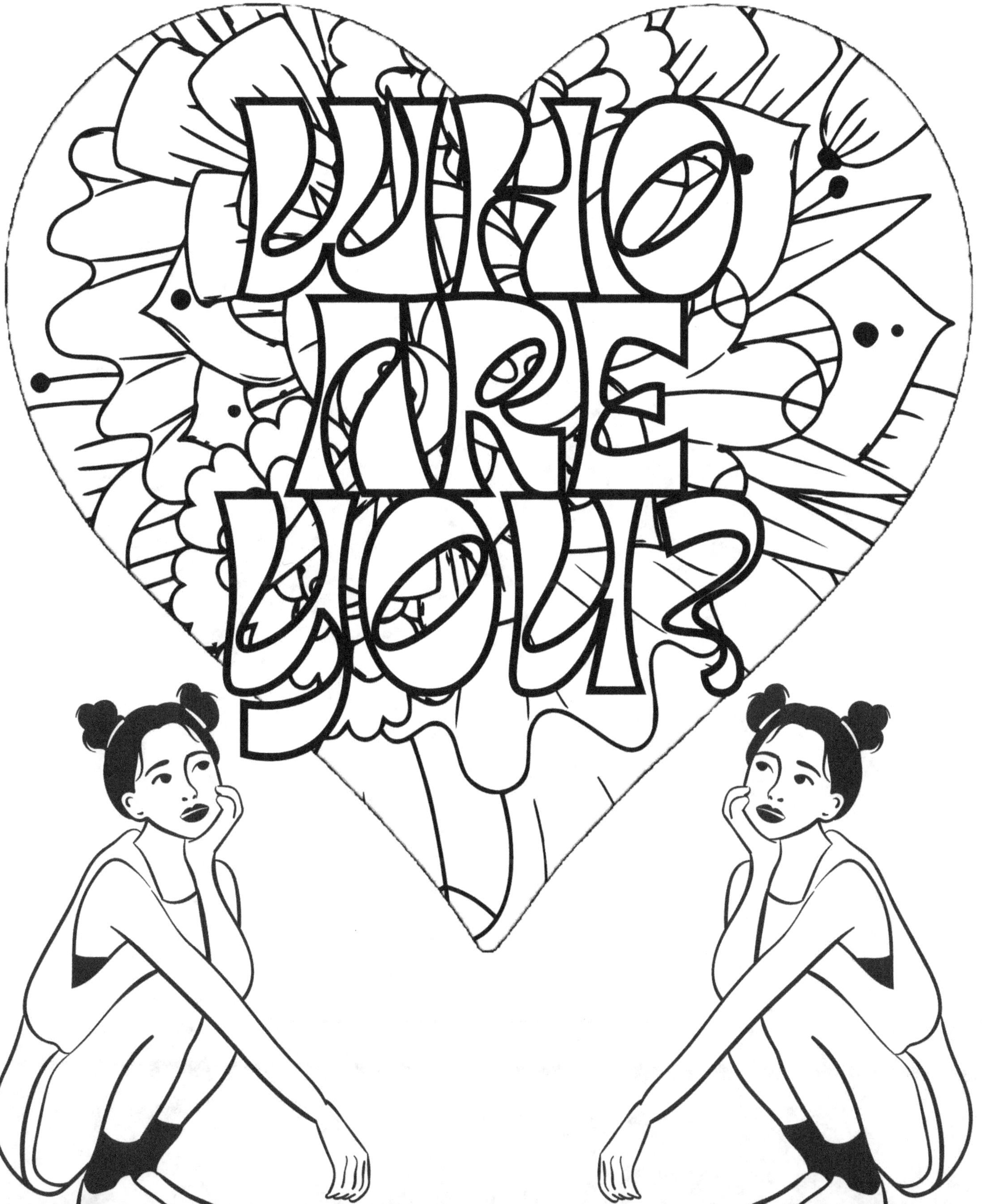
WHO ARE YOU?

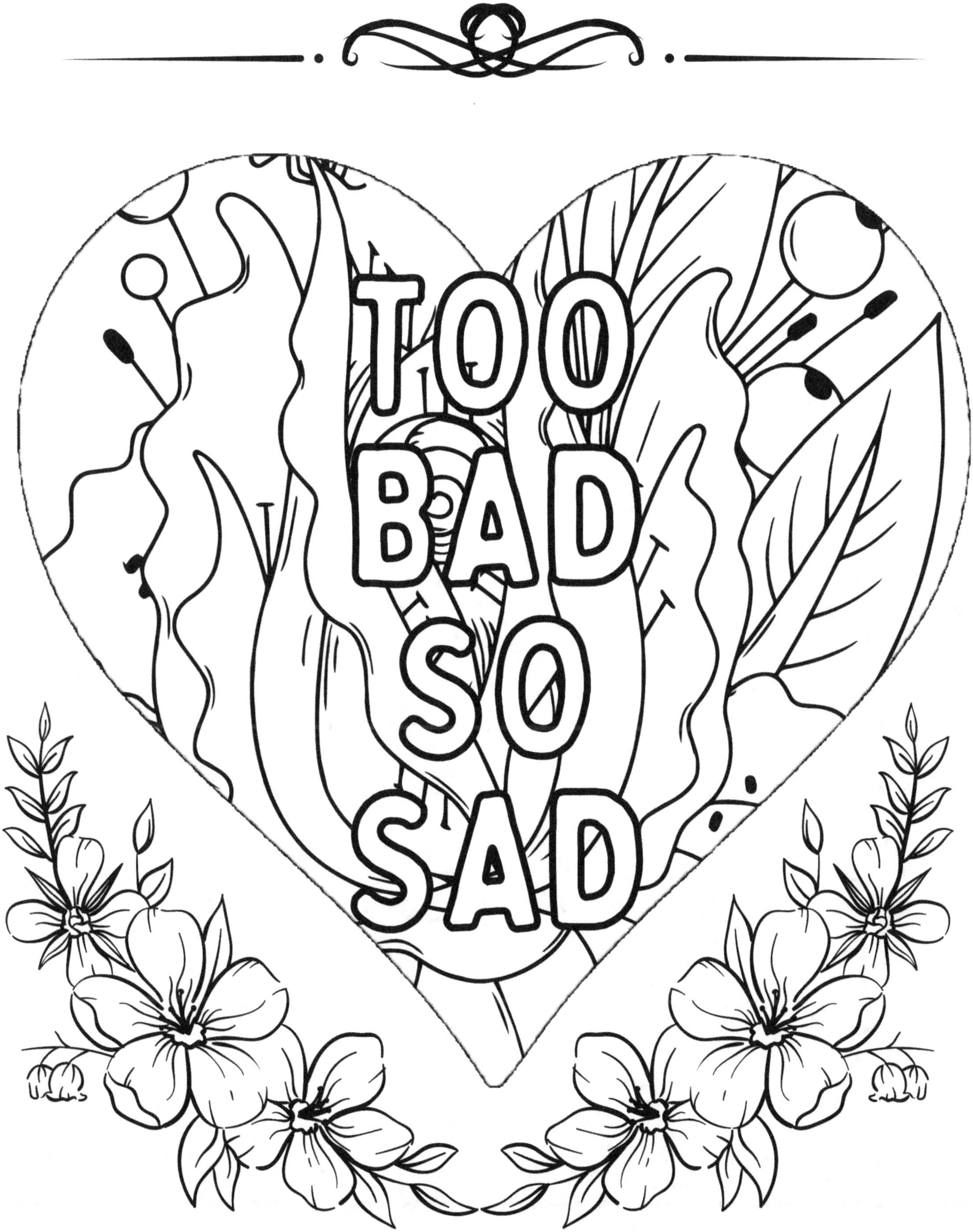
TOO
BAD
SO
SAD

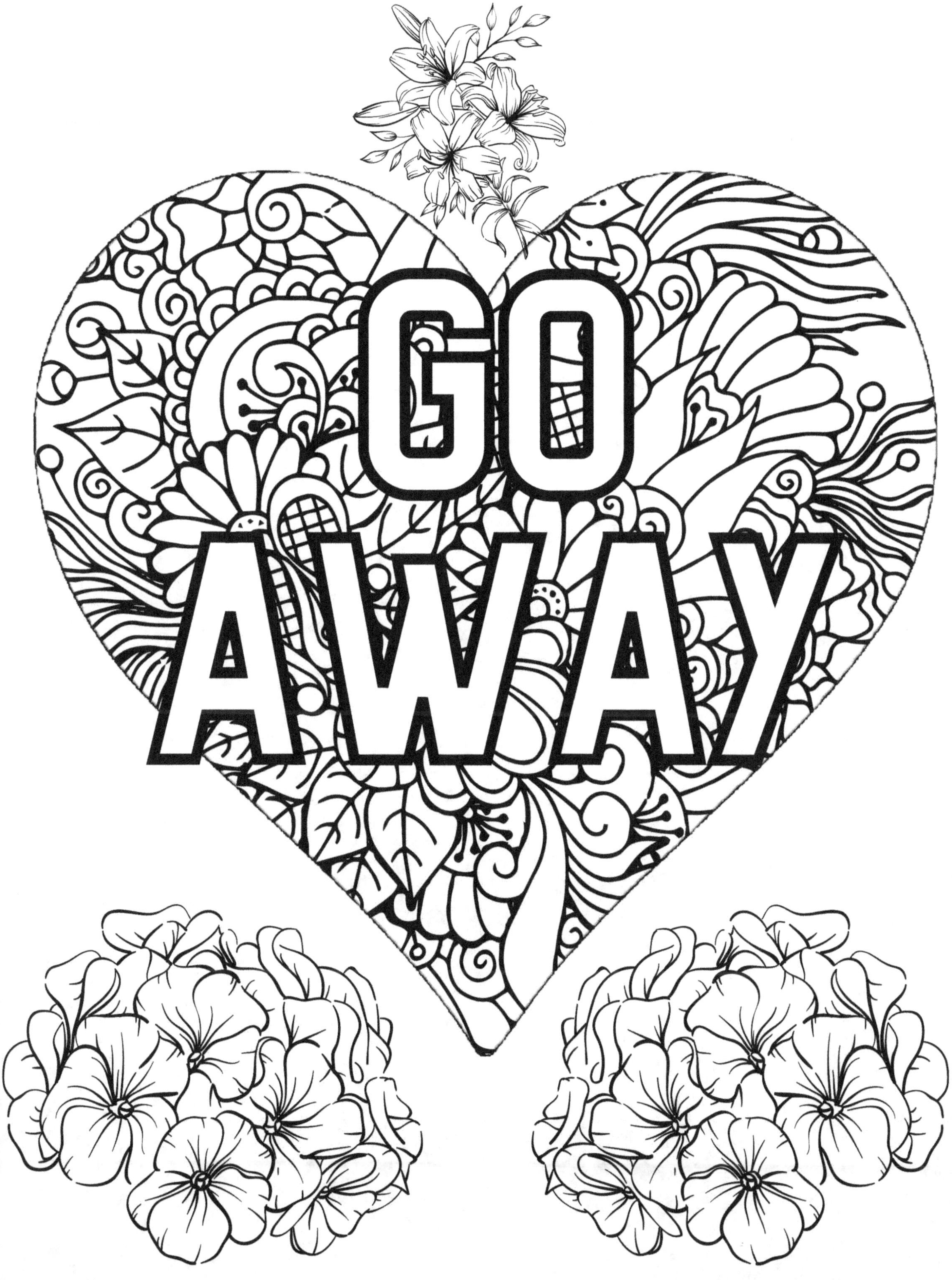
GO
AWAY

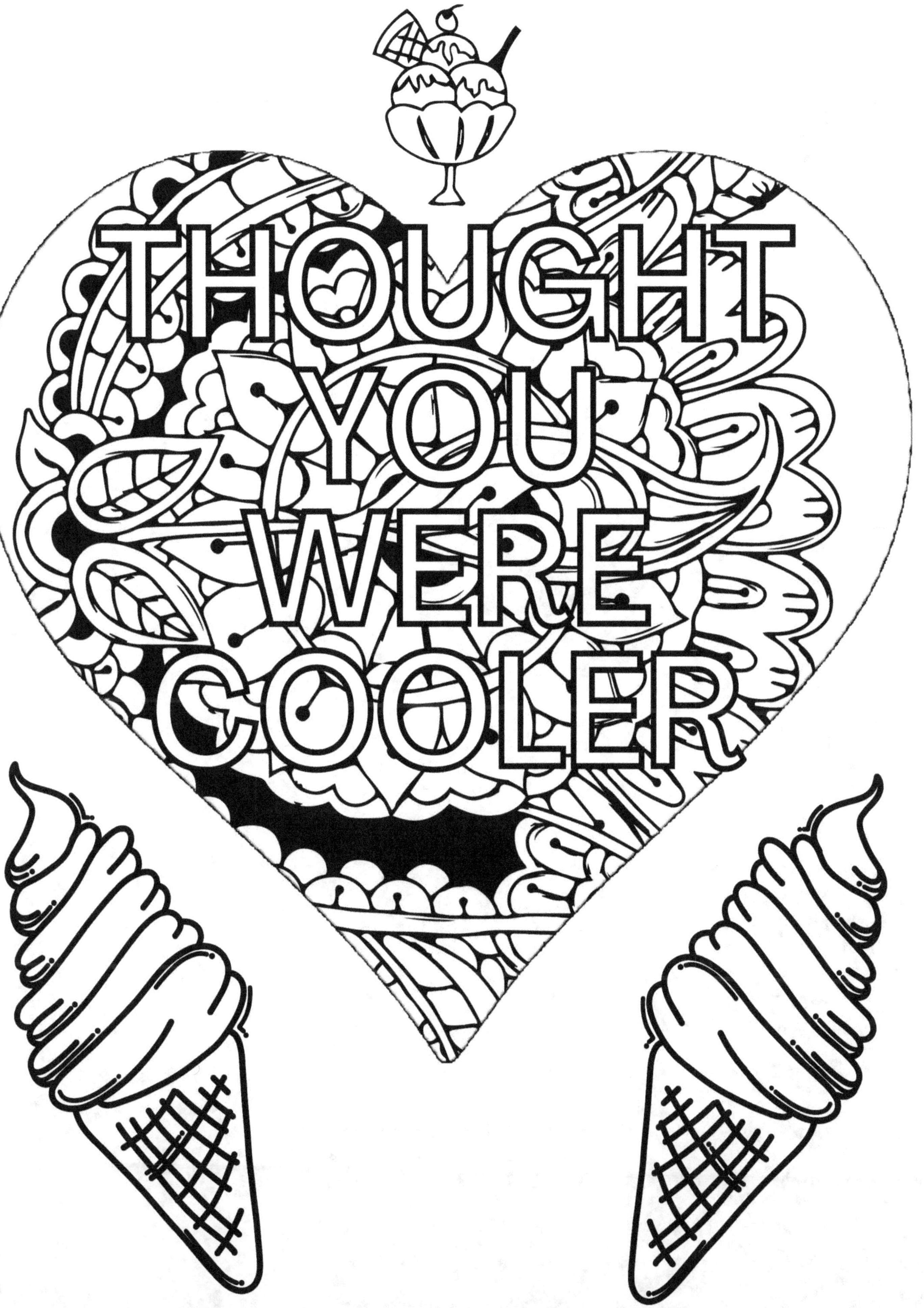
THOUGHT
YOU
WERE
COOLER

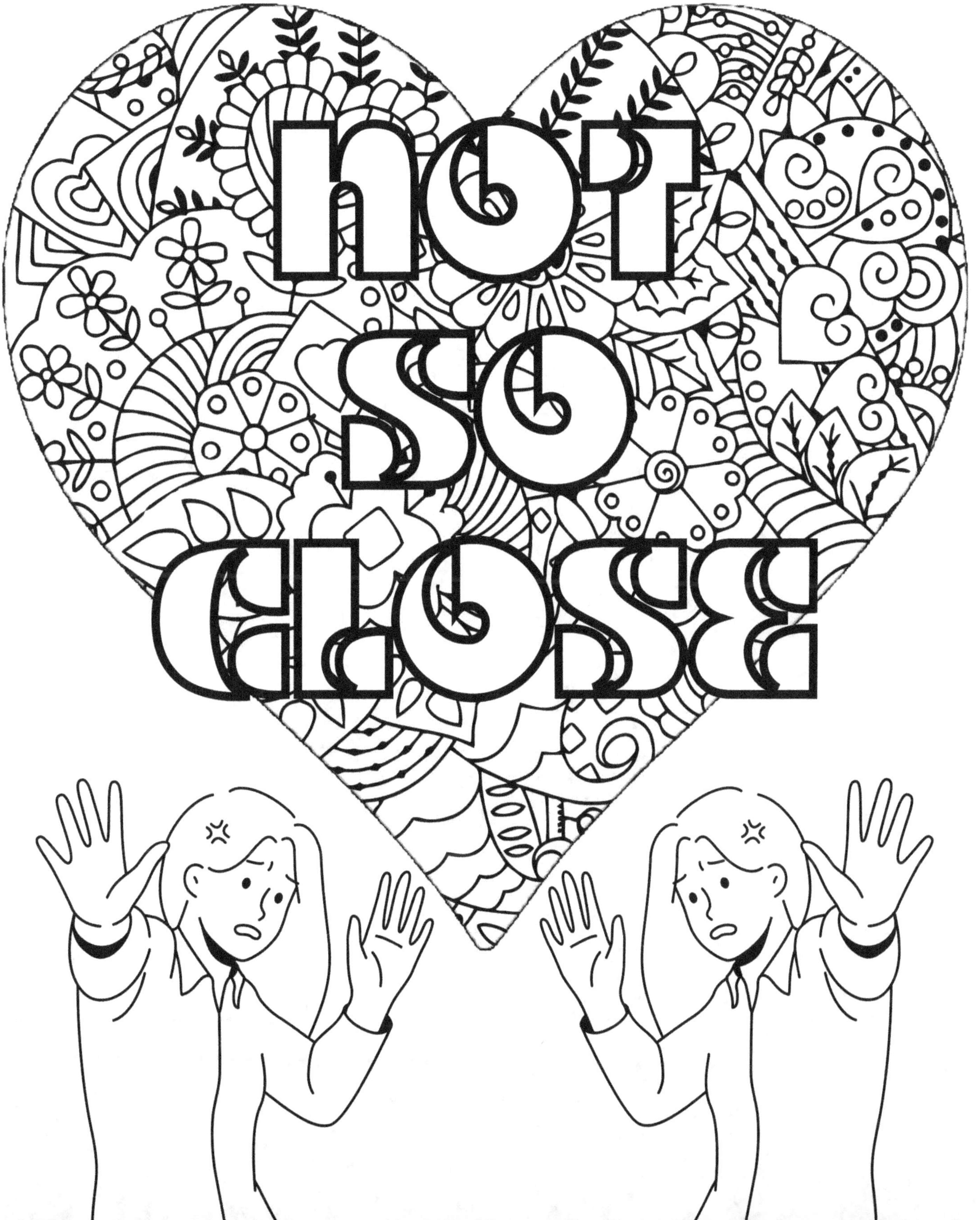
NOT
SO
CLOSE

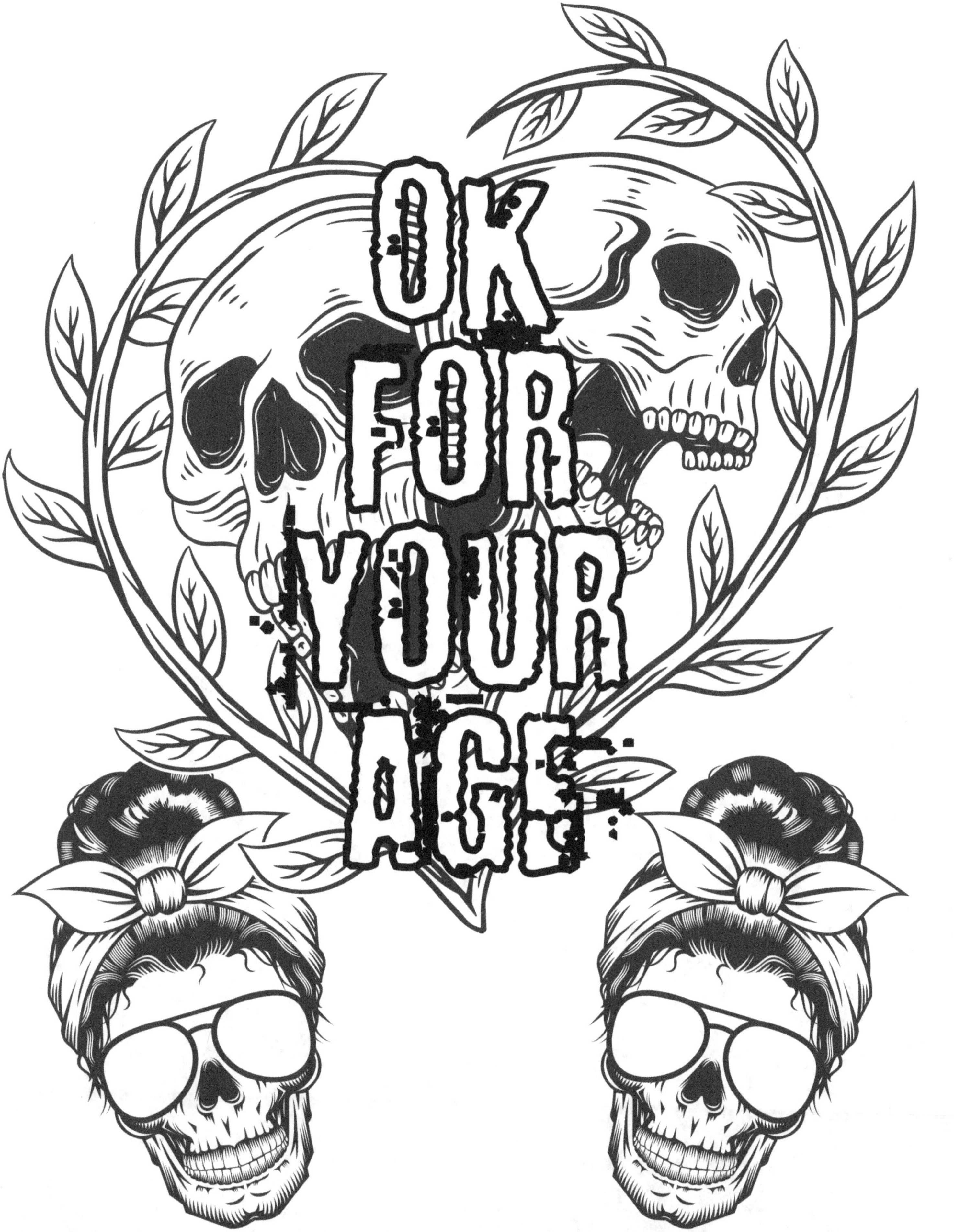
OK
FOR
YOUR
AGE

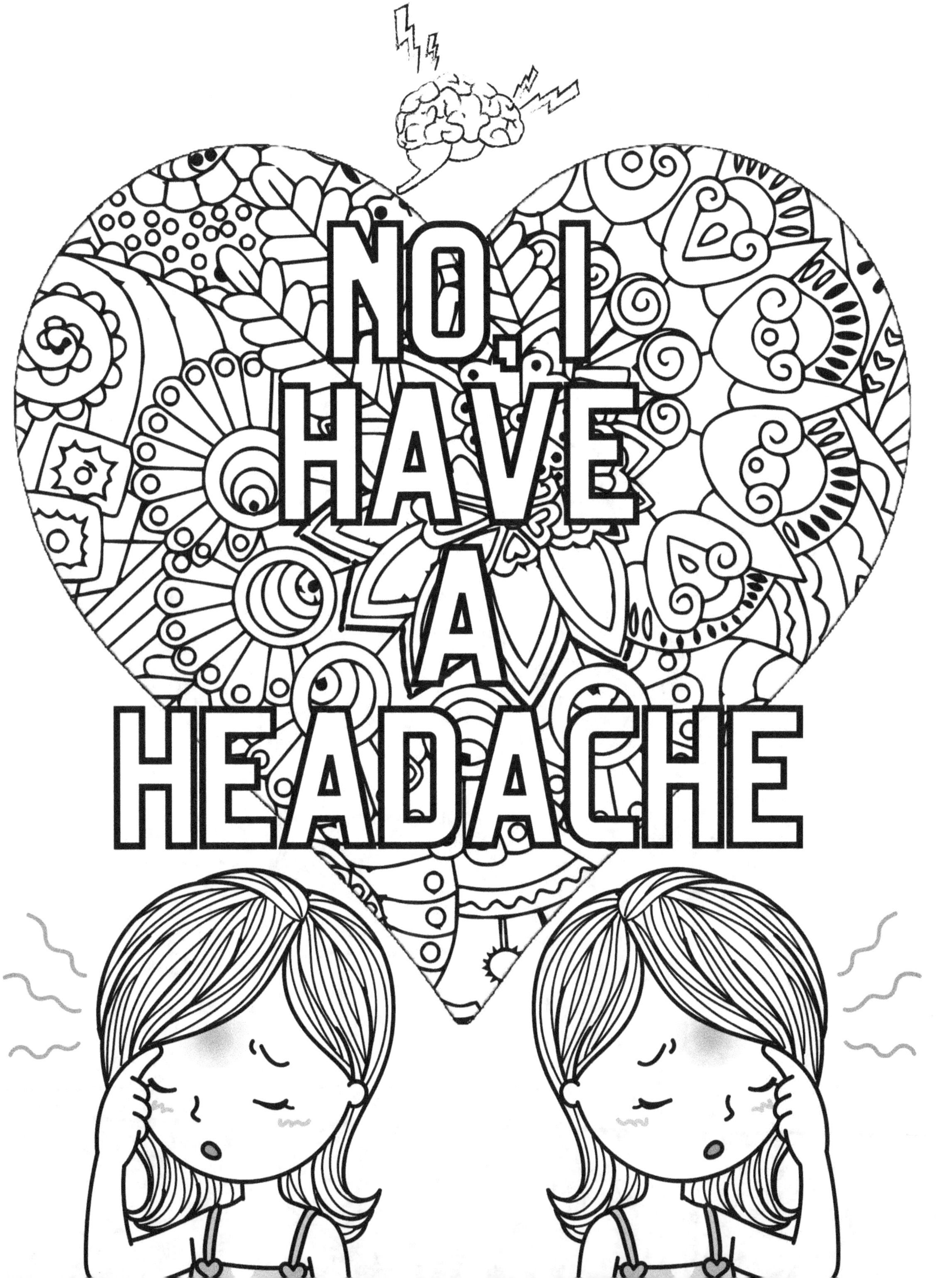
NO, I
HAVE
A
HEADACHE

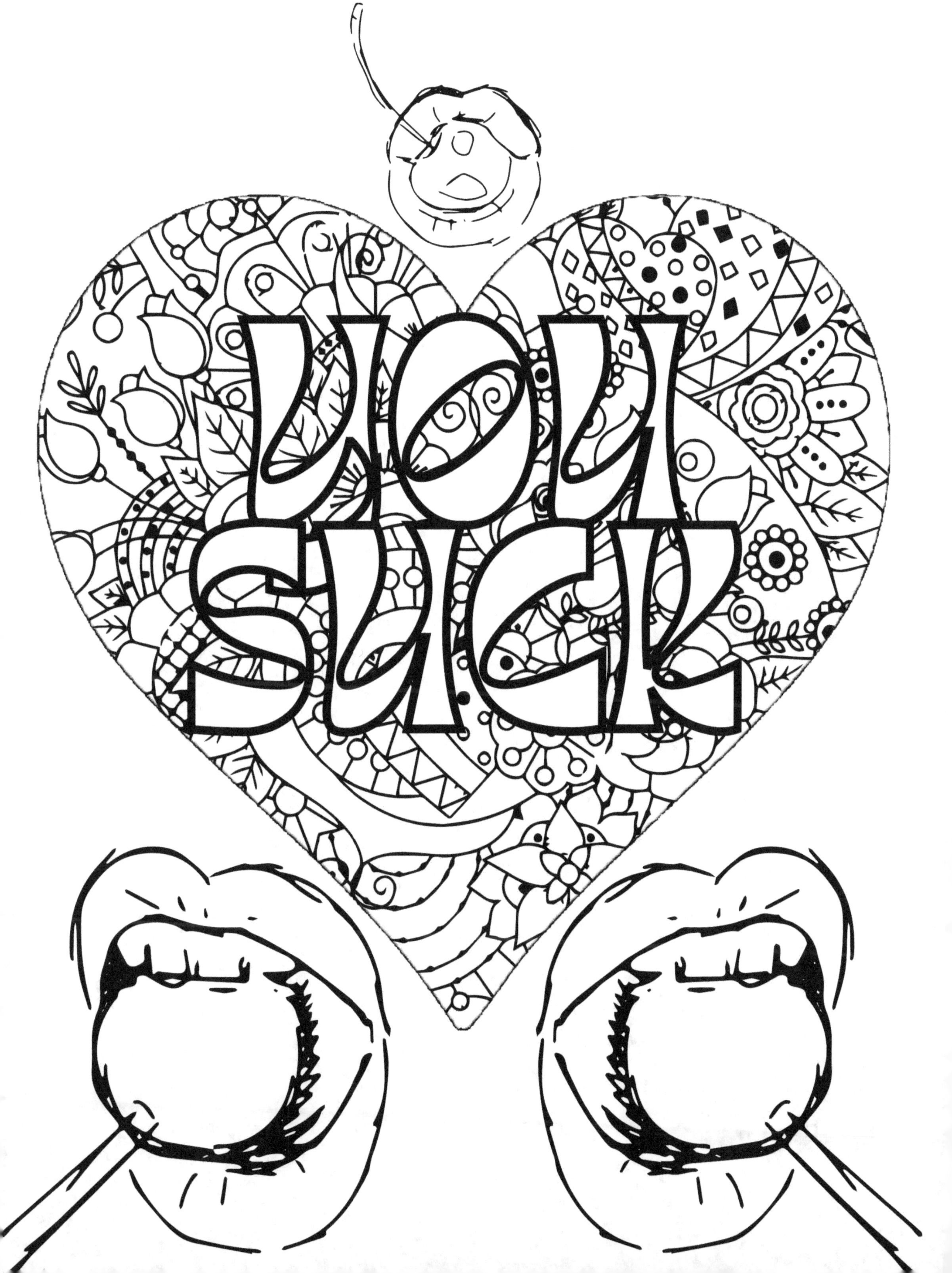
YOU
SUCK

NOT
TONIGHT

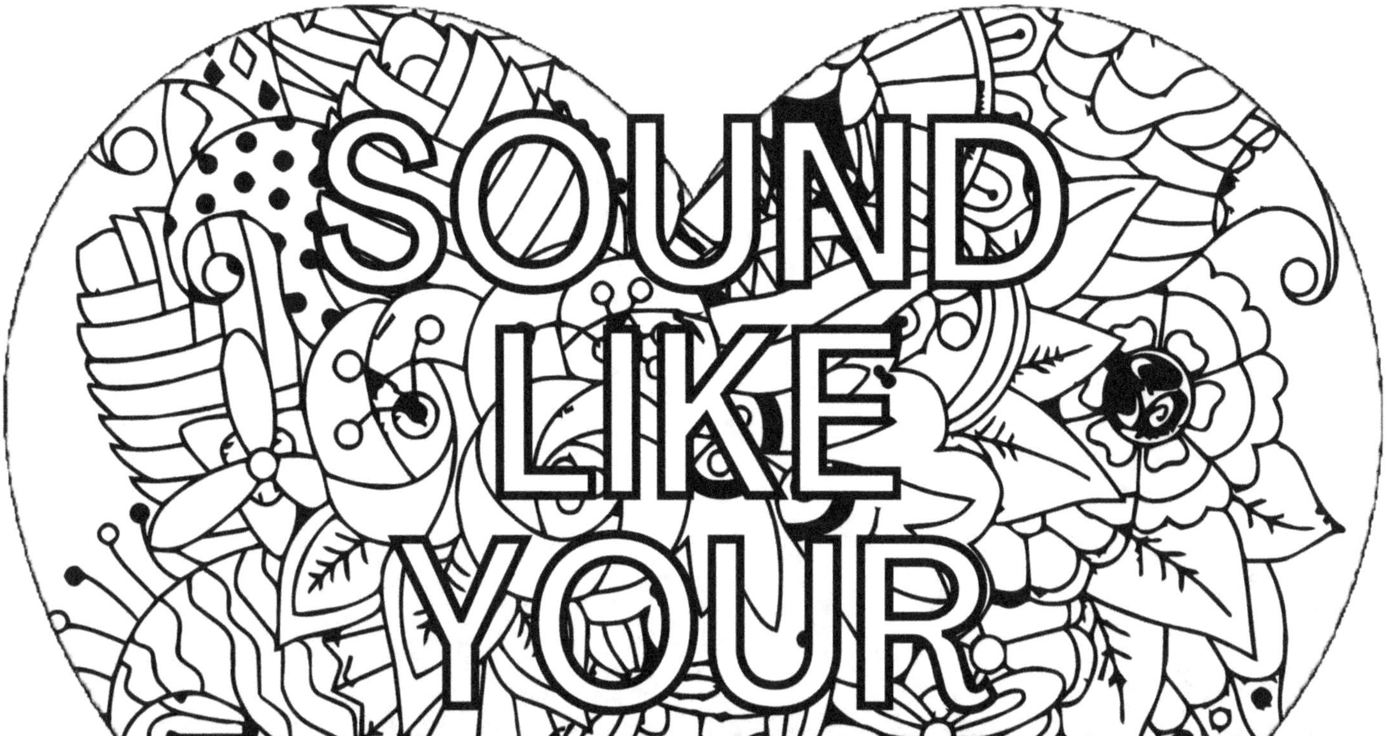
SOUND
LIKE
YOUR
MOTHER

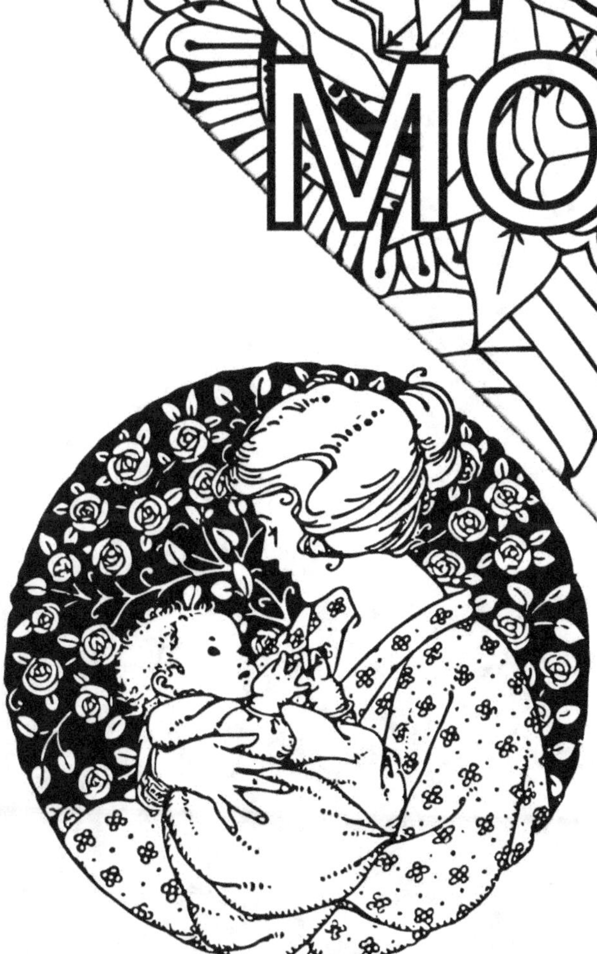

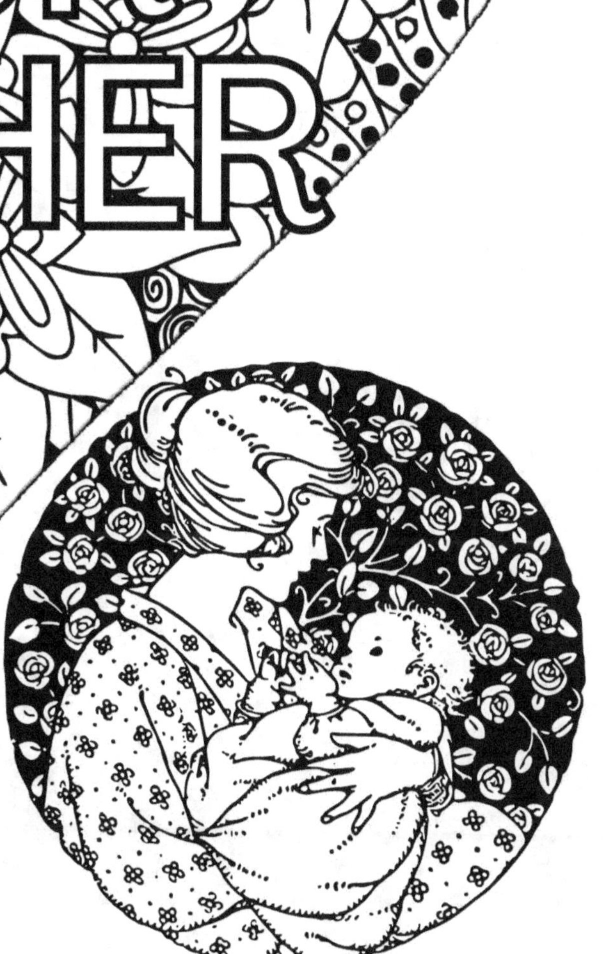

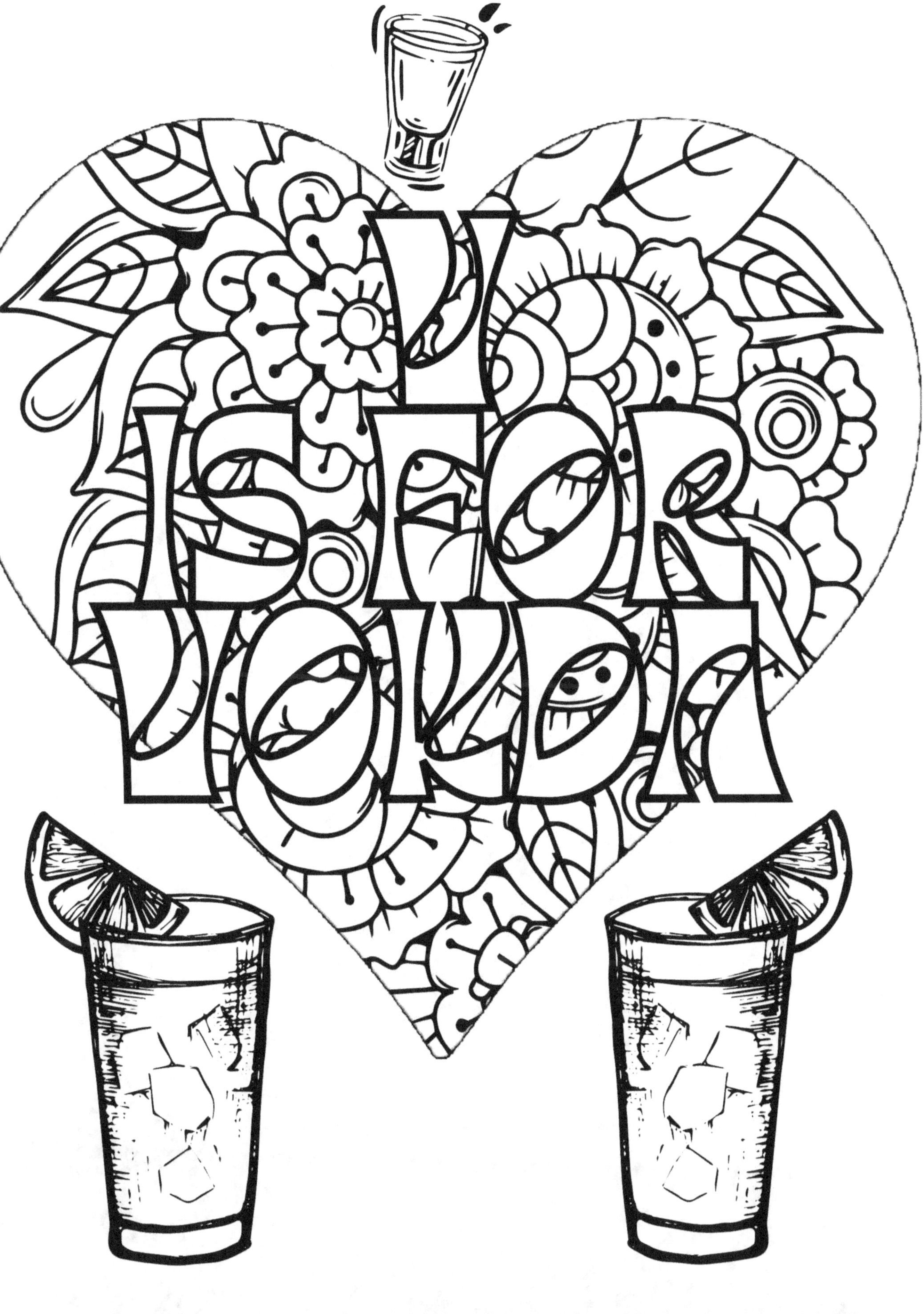
V
IS FOR
VODKA

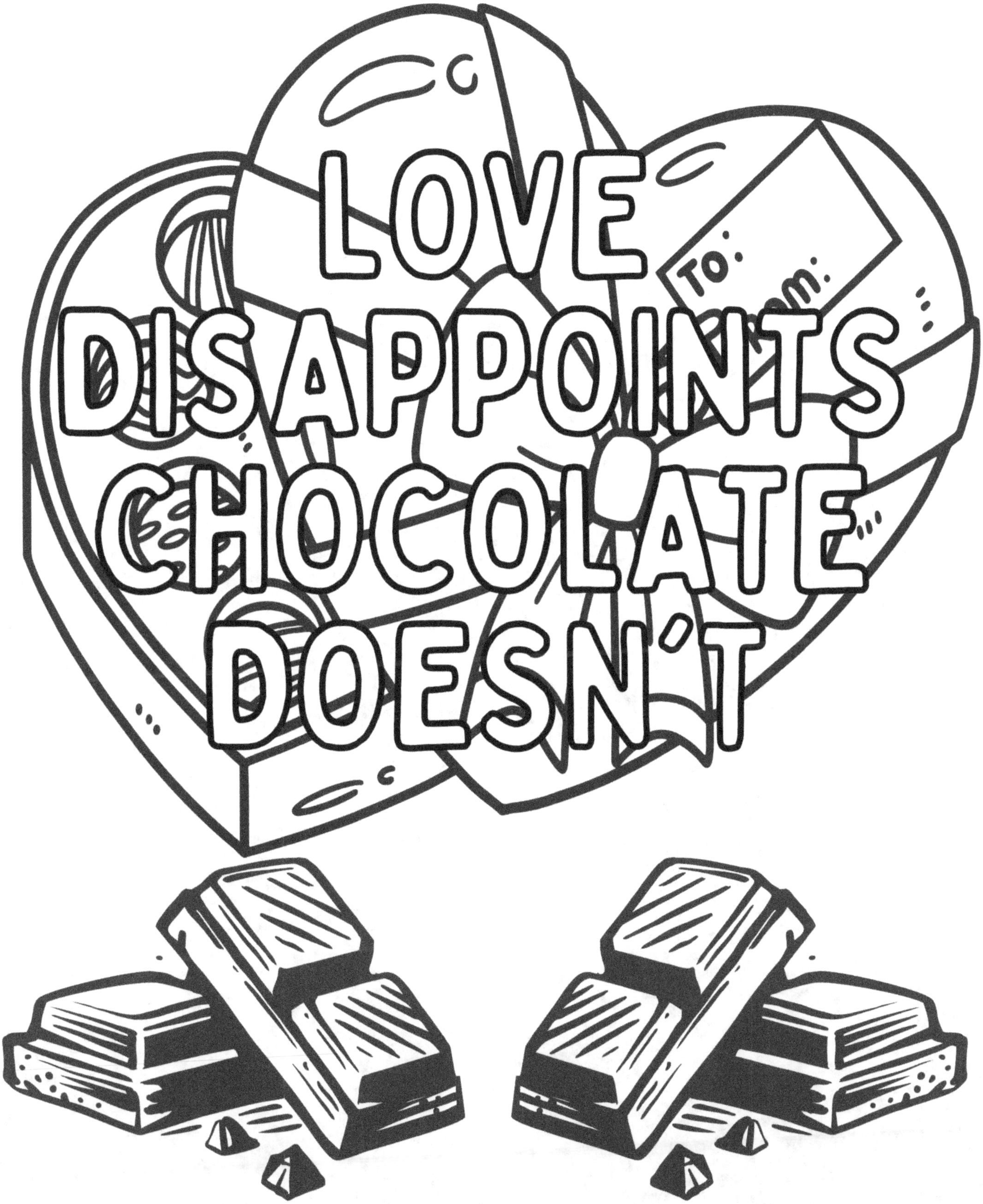
LOVE
DISAPPOINTS
CHOCOLATE
DOESN'T
To:

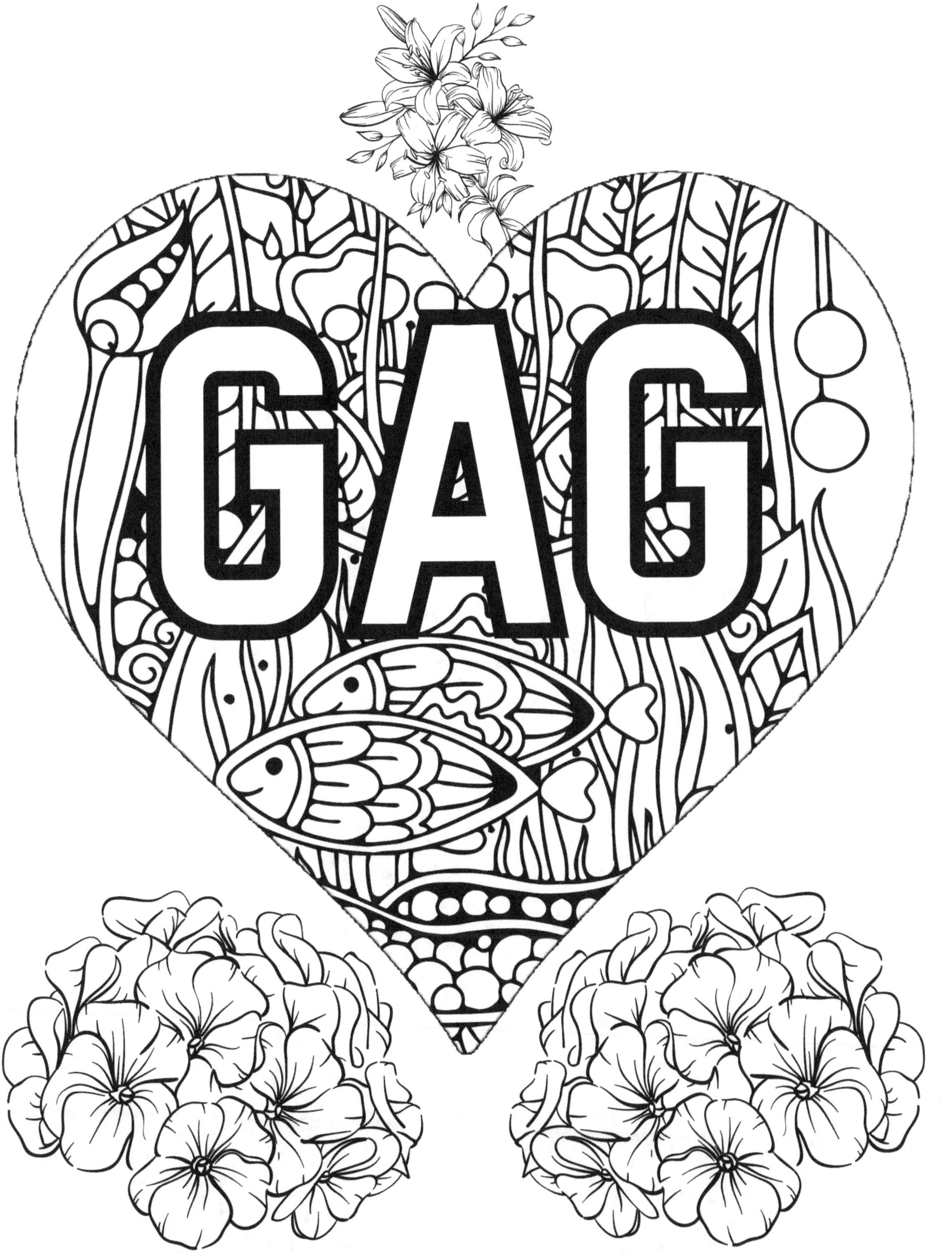
GAG

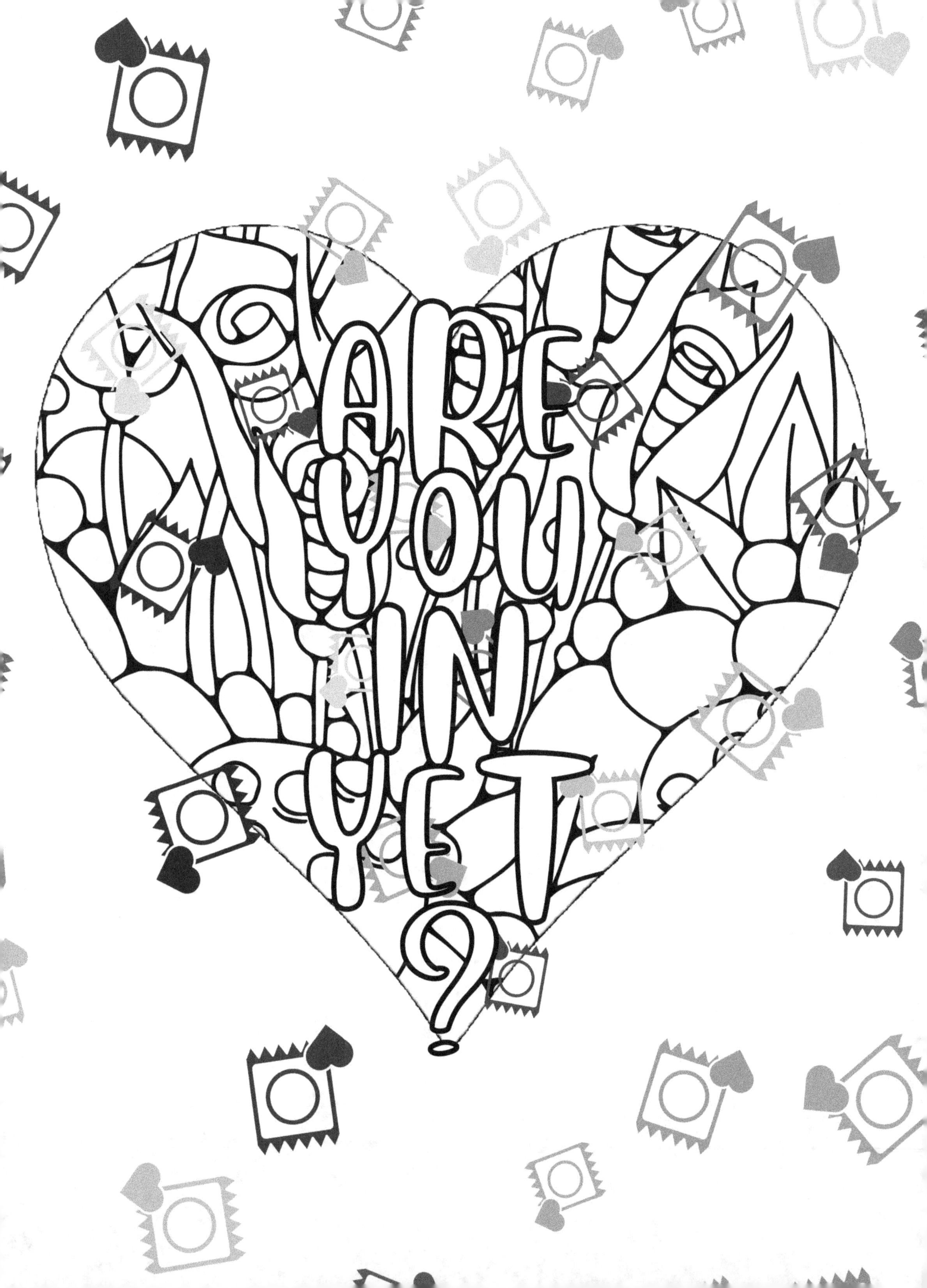
ARE YOU IN YET?

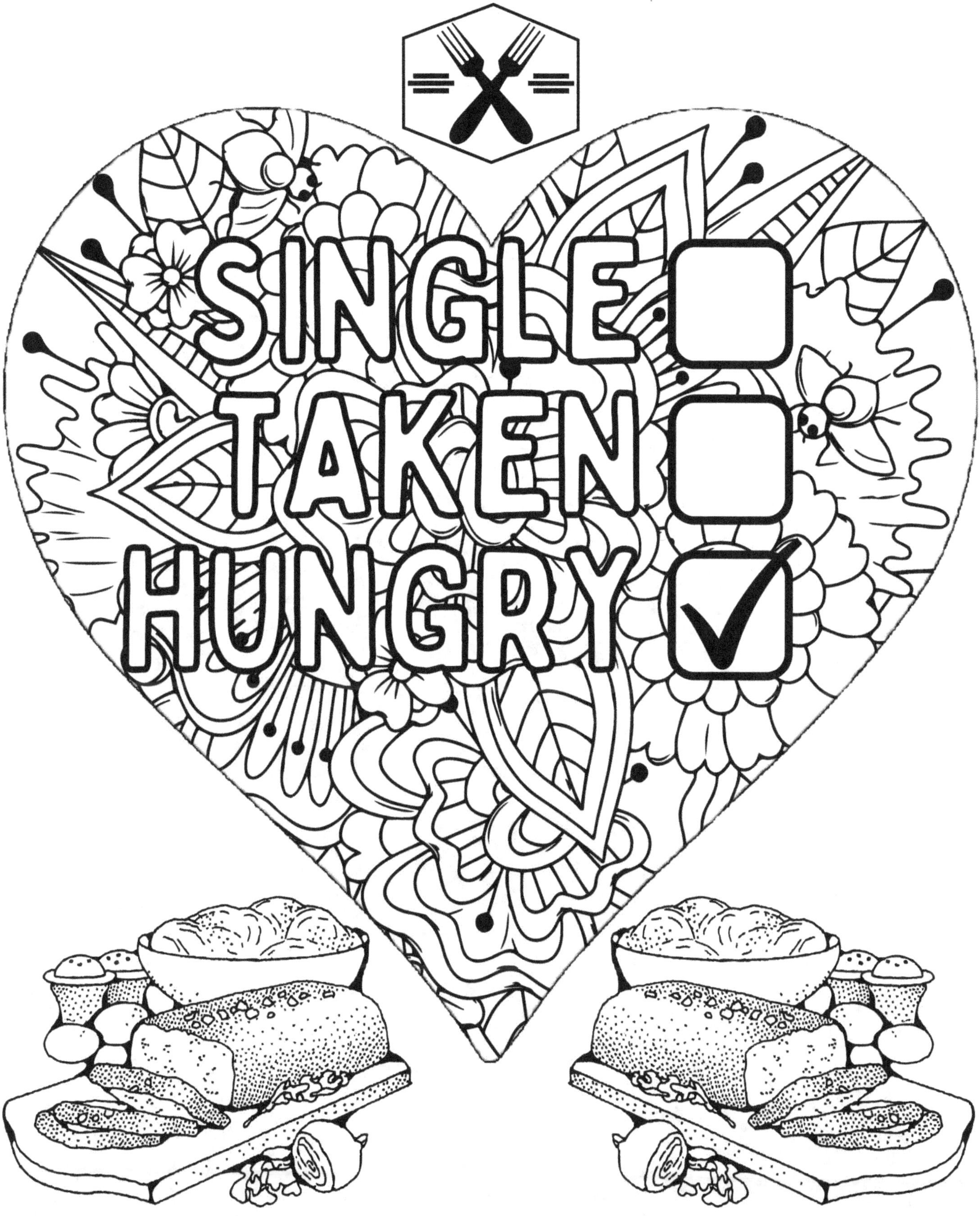
SINGLE
TAKEN
HUNGRY

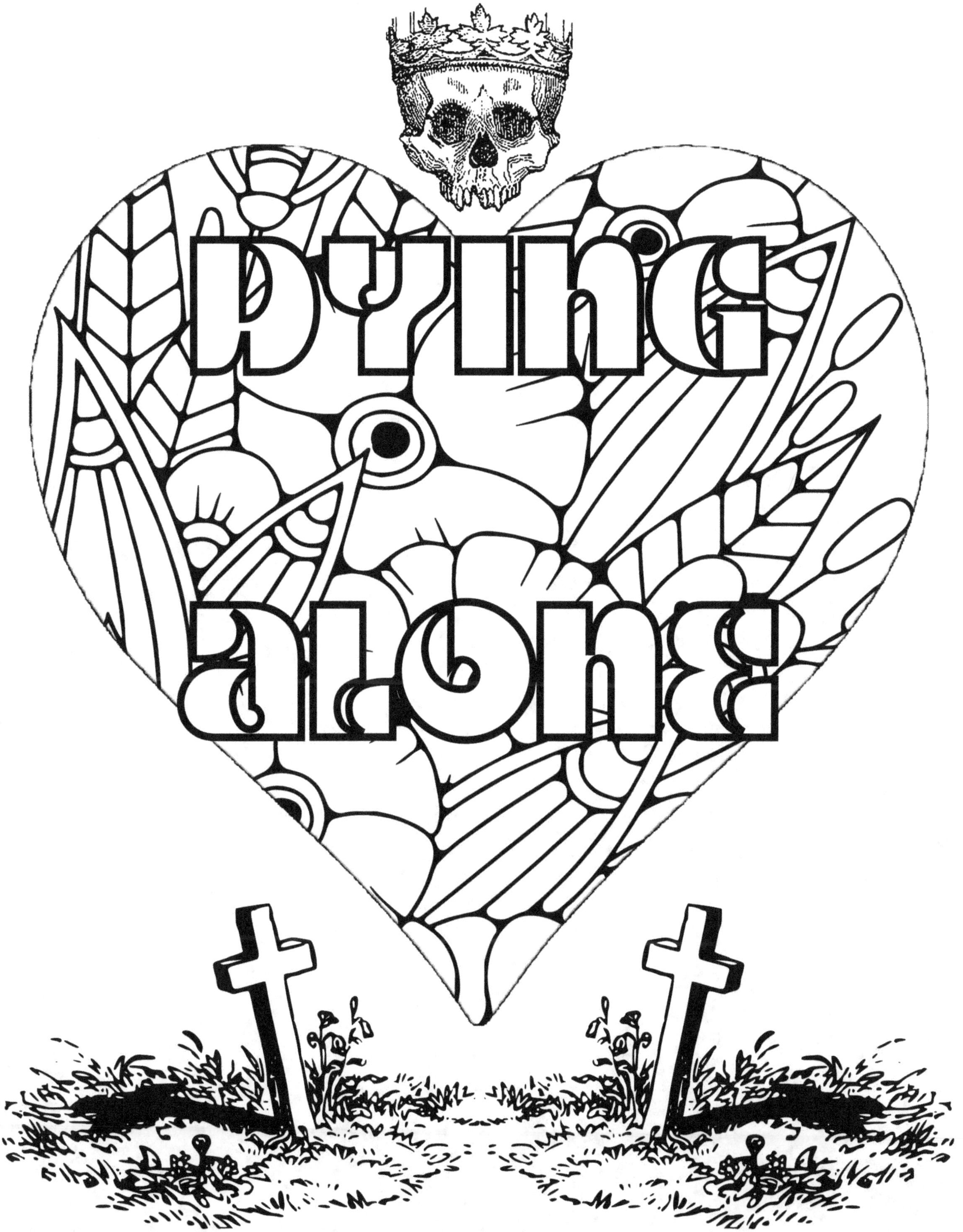
DYING
ALONE

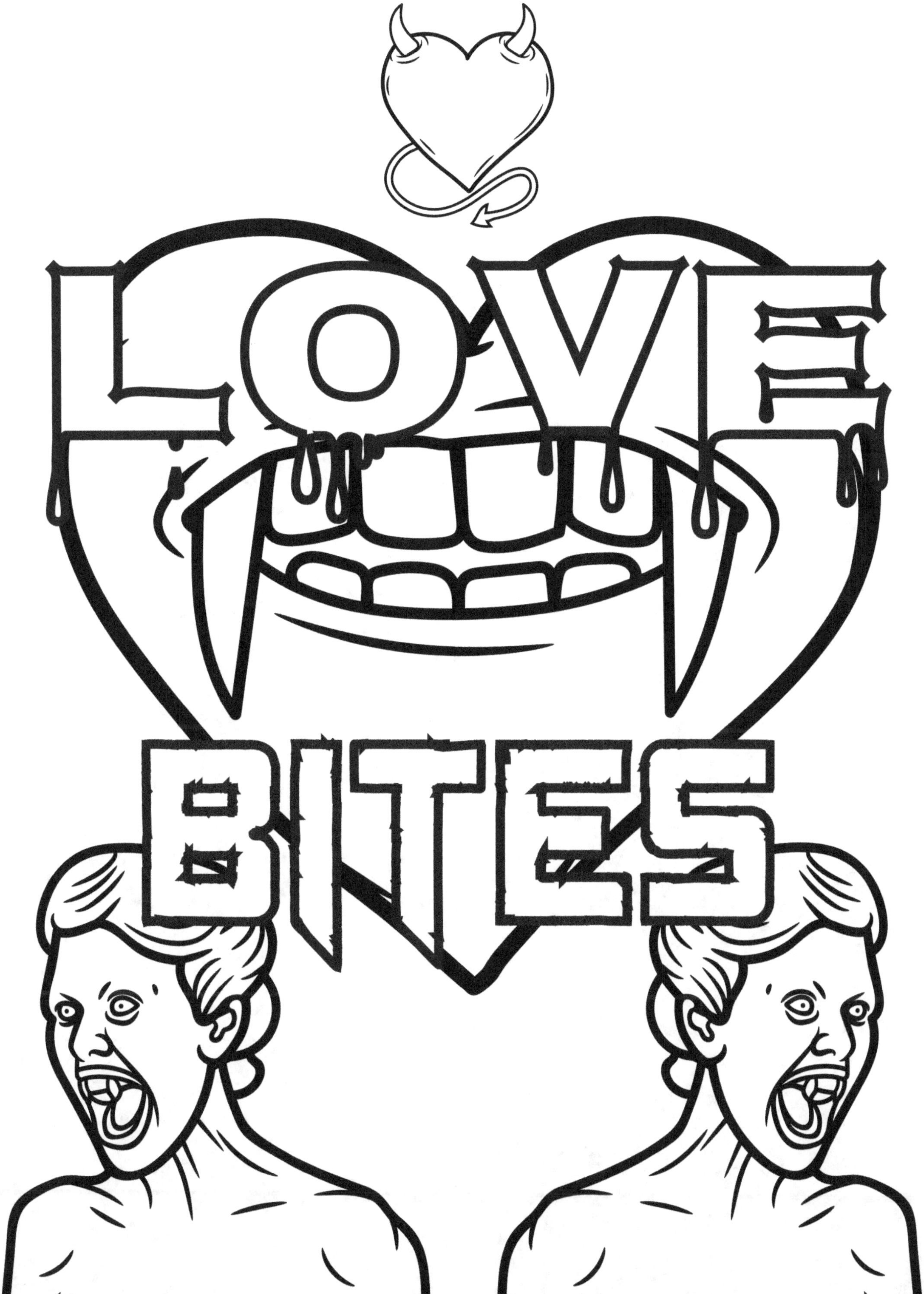
LOVE
BITES

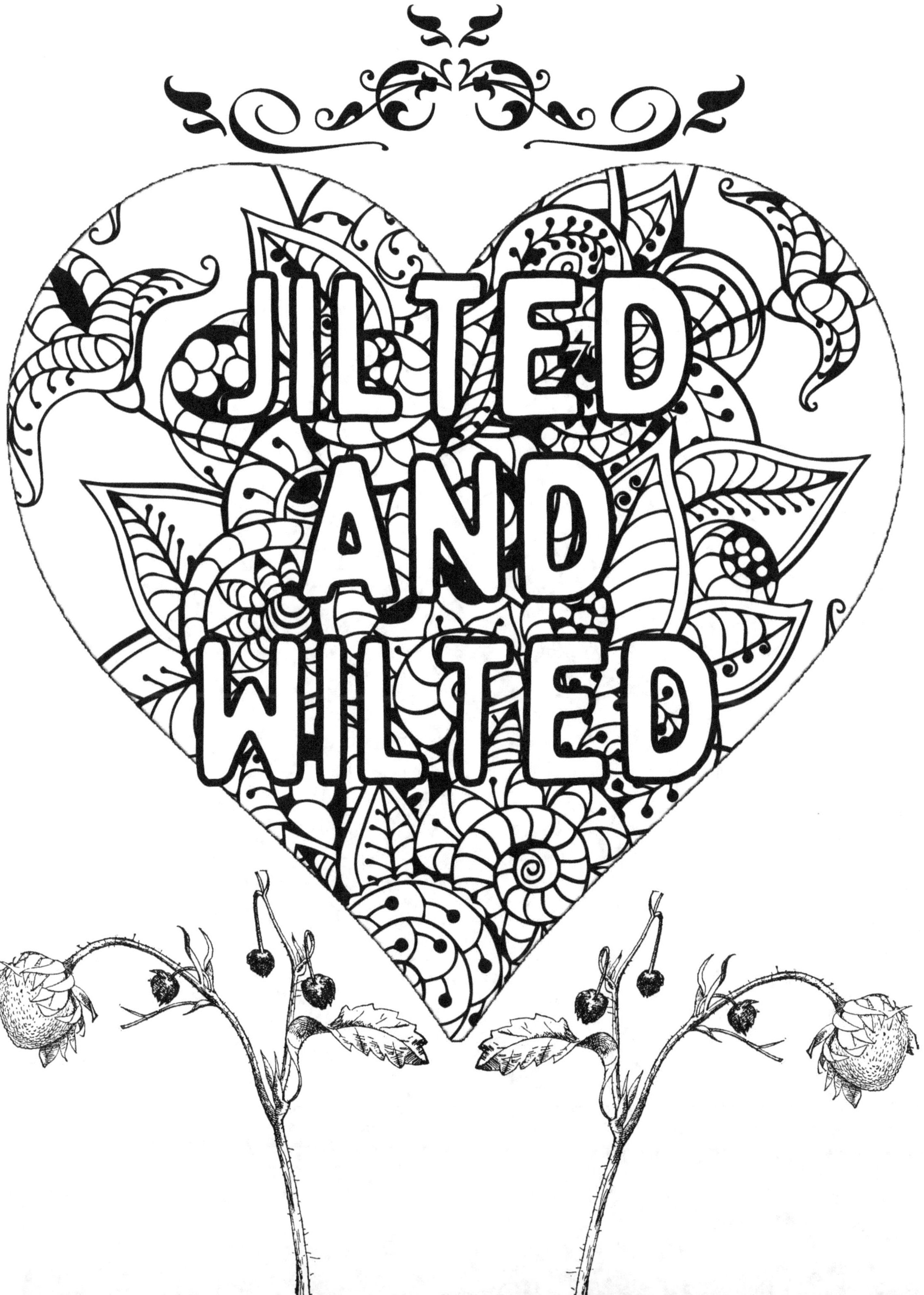
JILTED
AND
WILTED

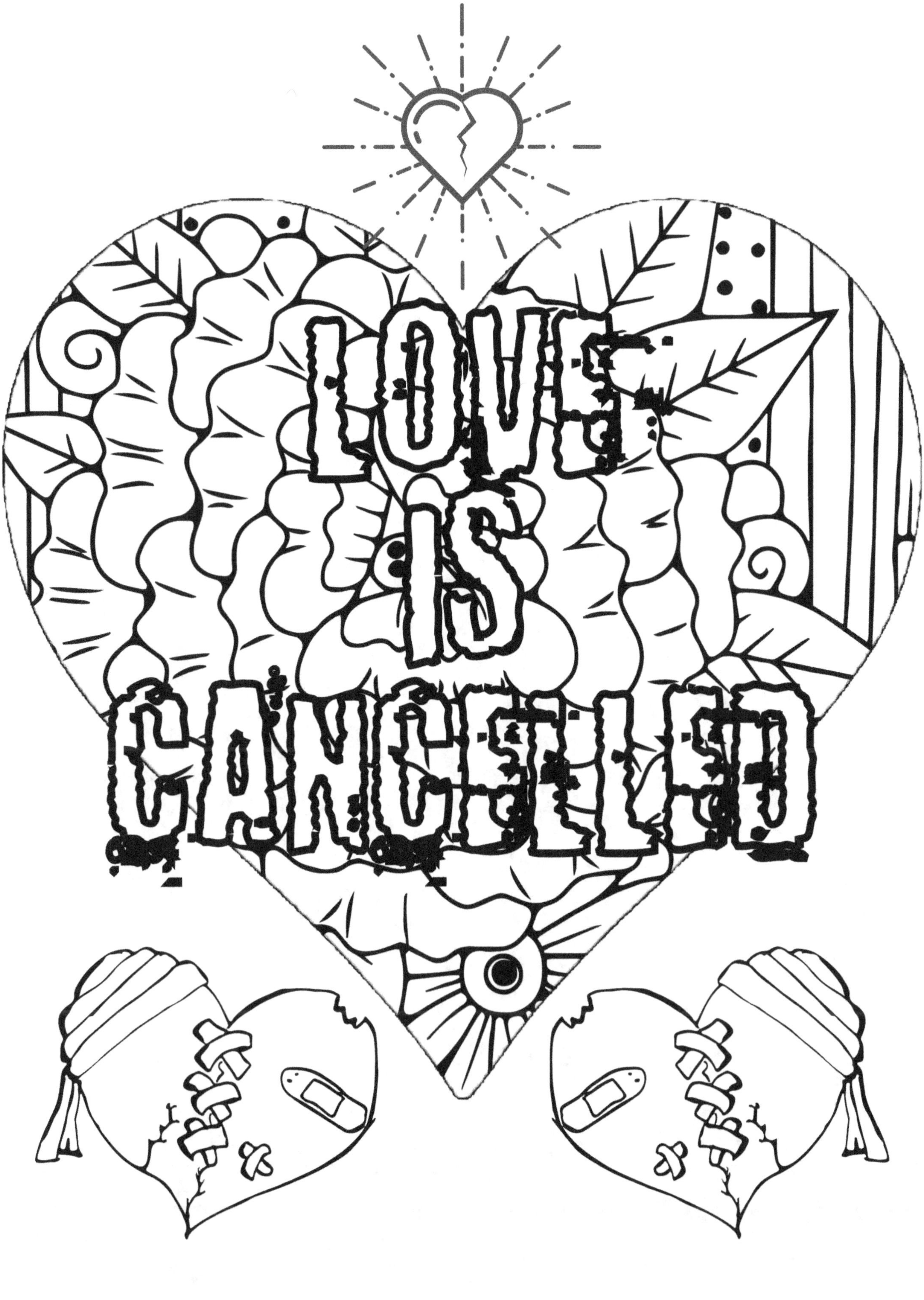
LOVE
IS
CANCELLED

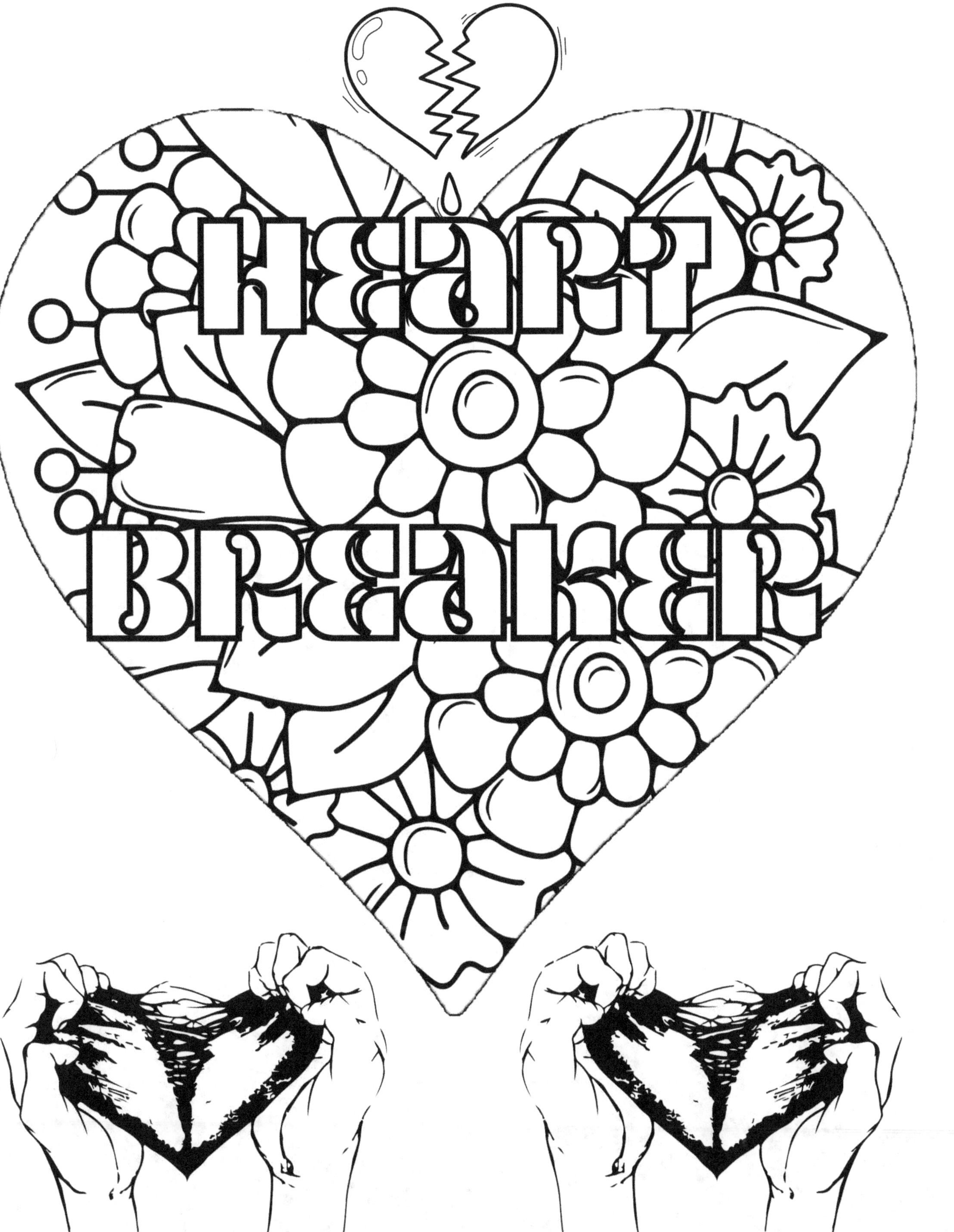
HEART
BREAKER

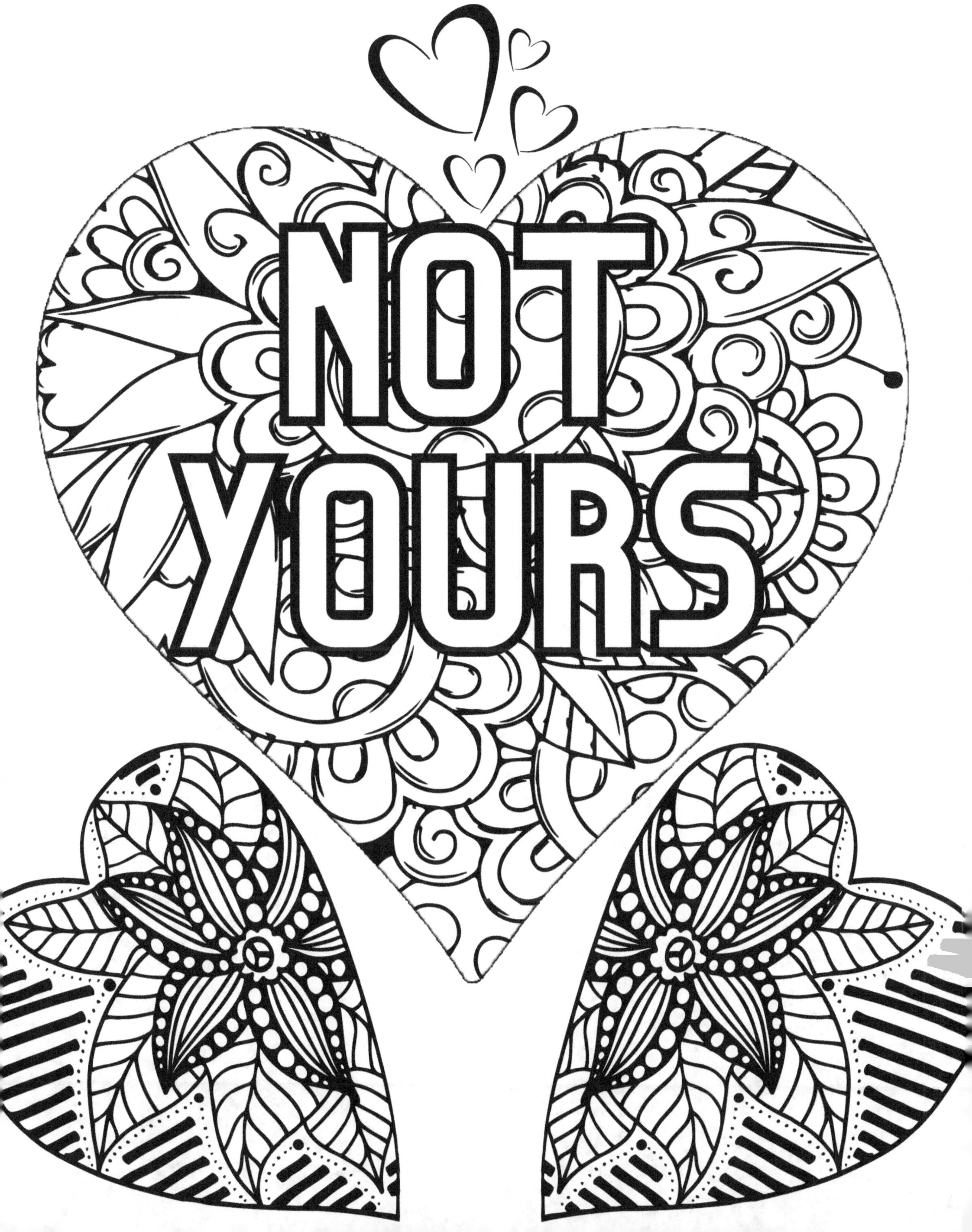
NOT
YOURS

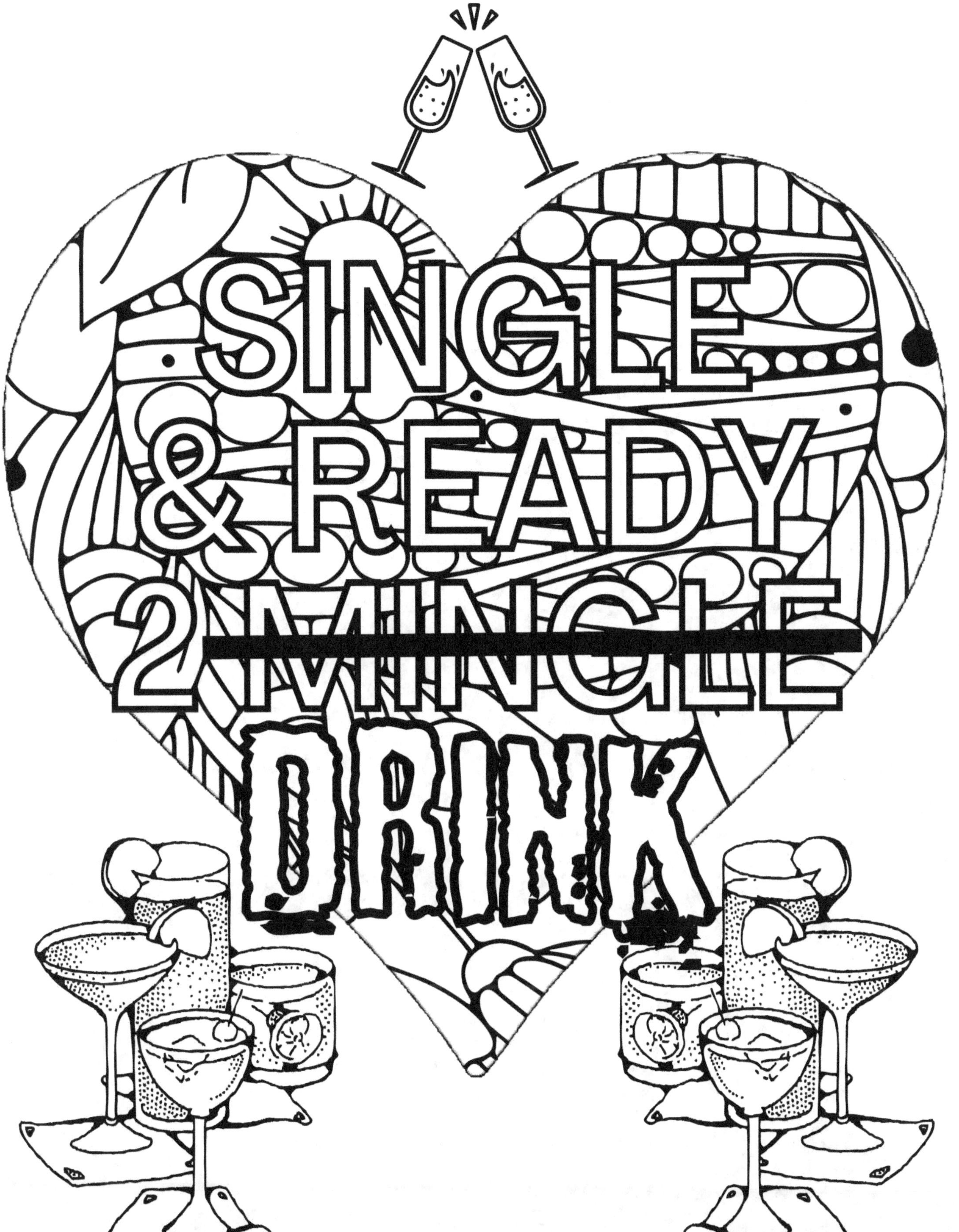
SINGLE
& READY
2 MINGLE
DRINK

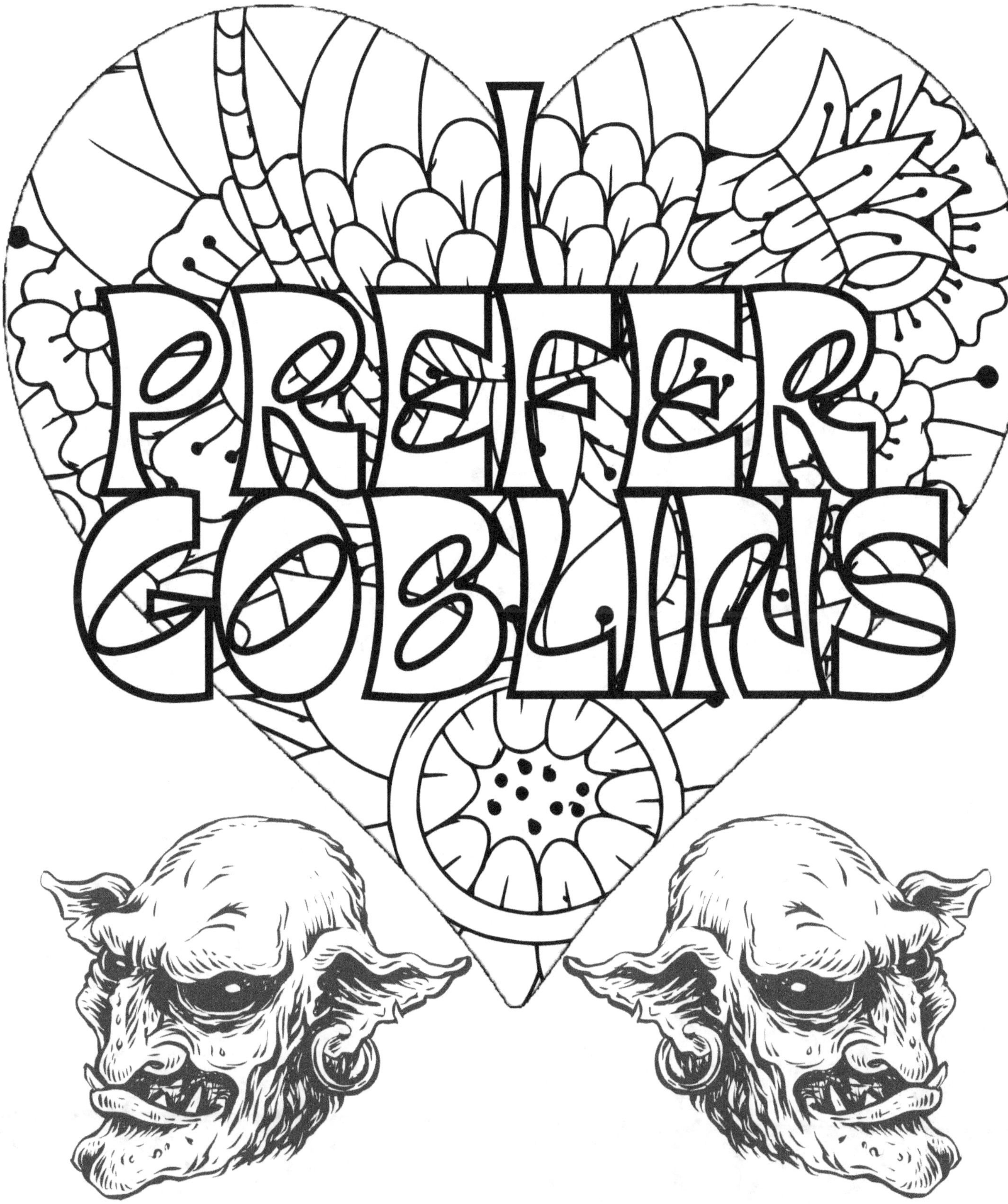
I
PREFER
GOBLINS

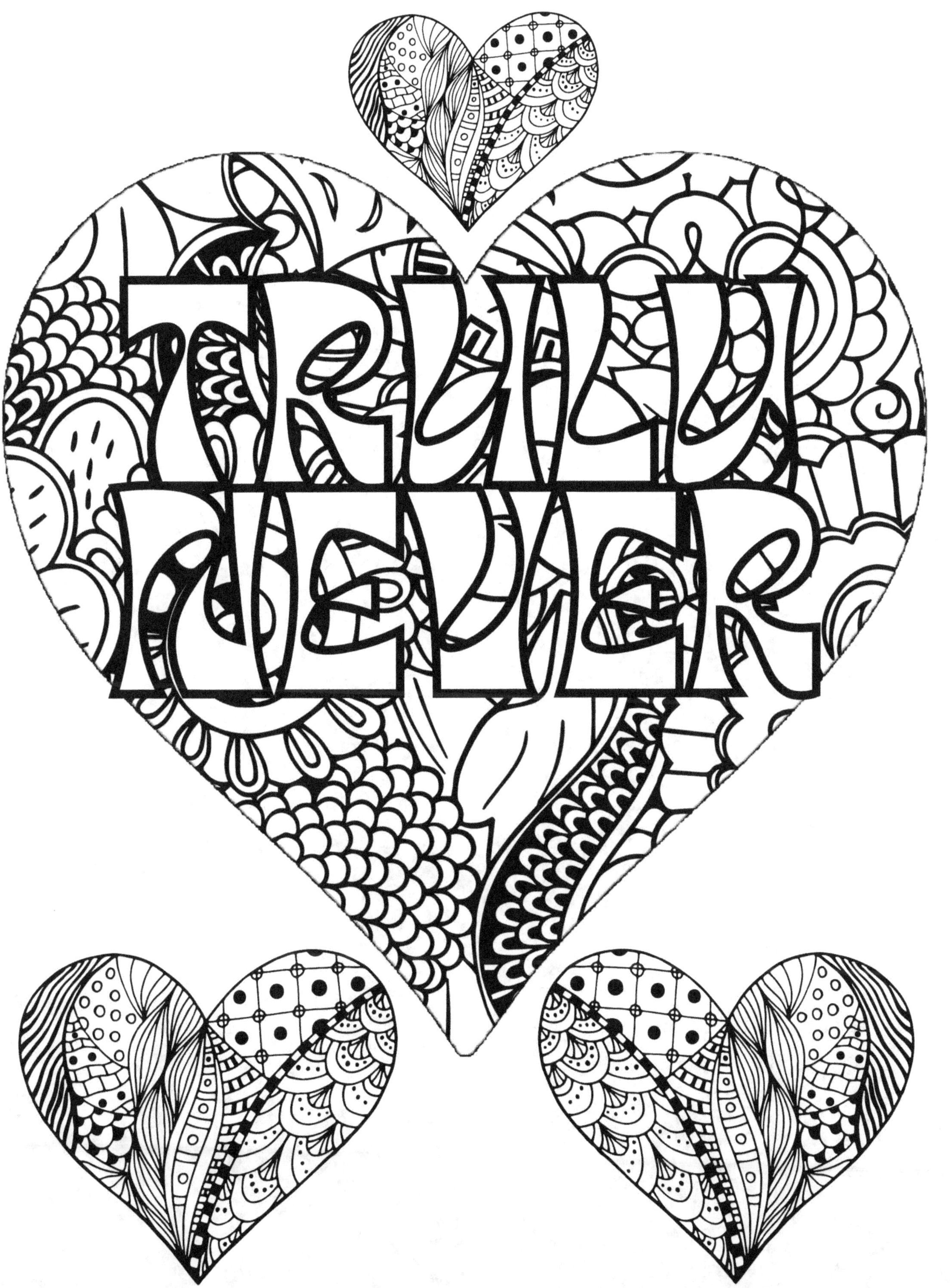
TRULY
CLEVER

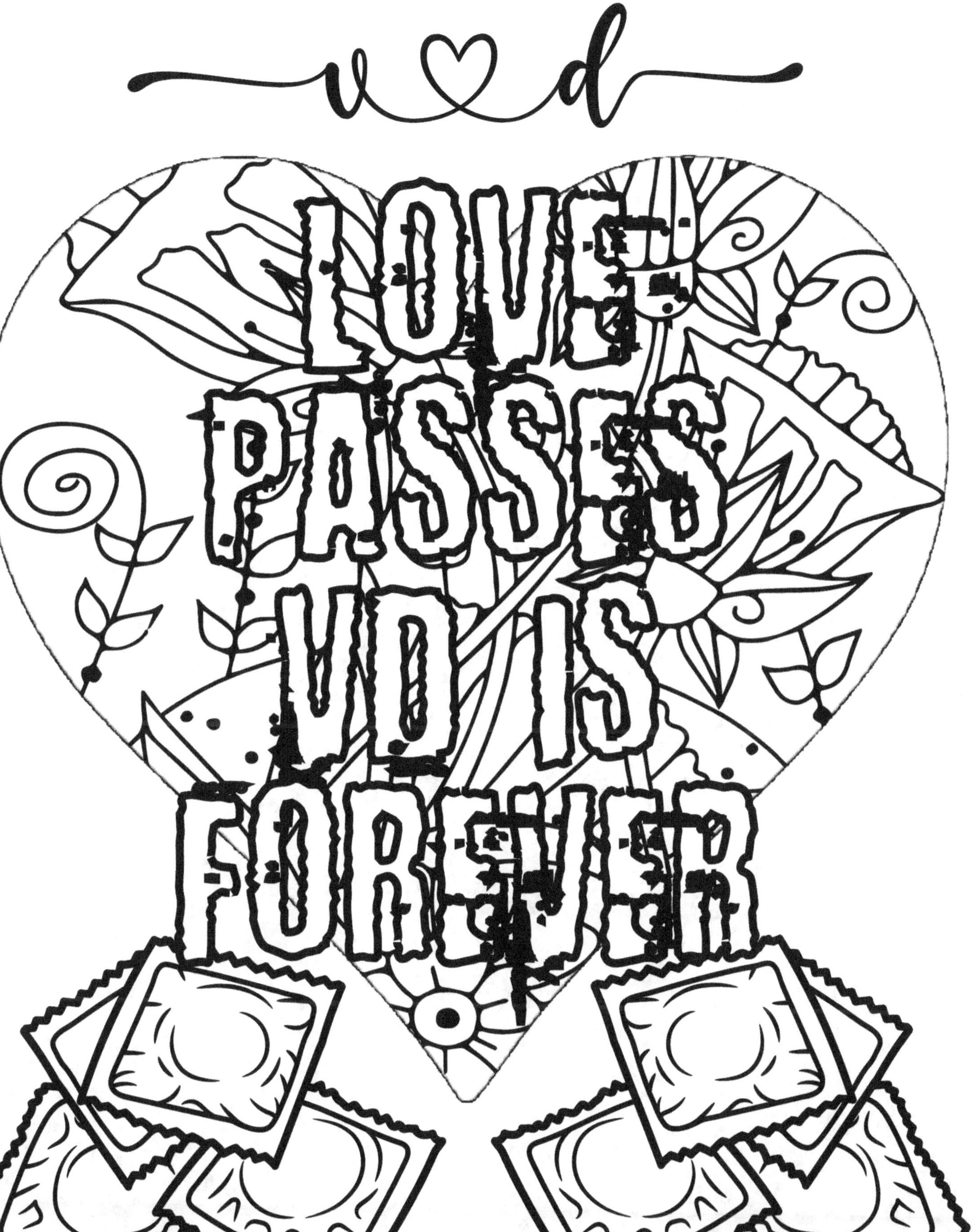
v d
LOVE
PASSES
VD IS
FOREVER

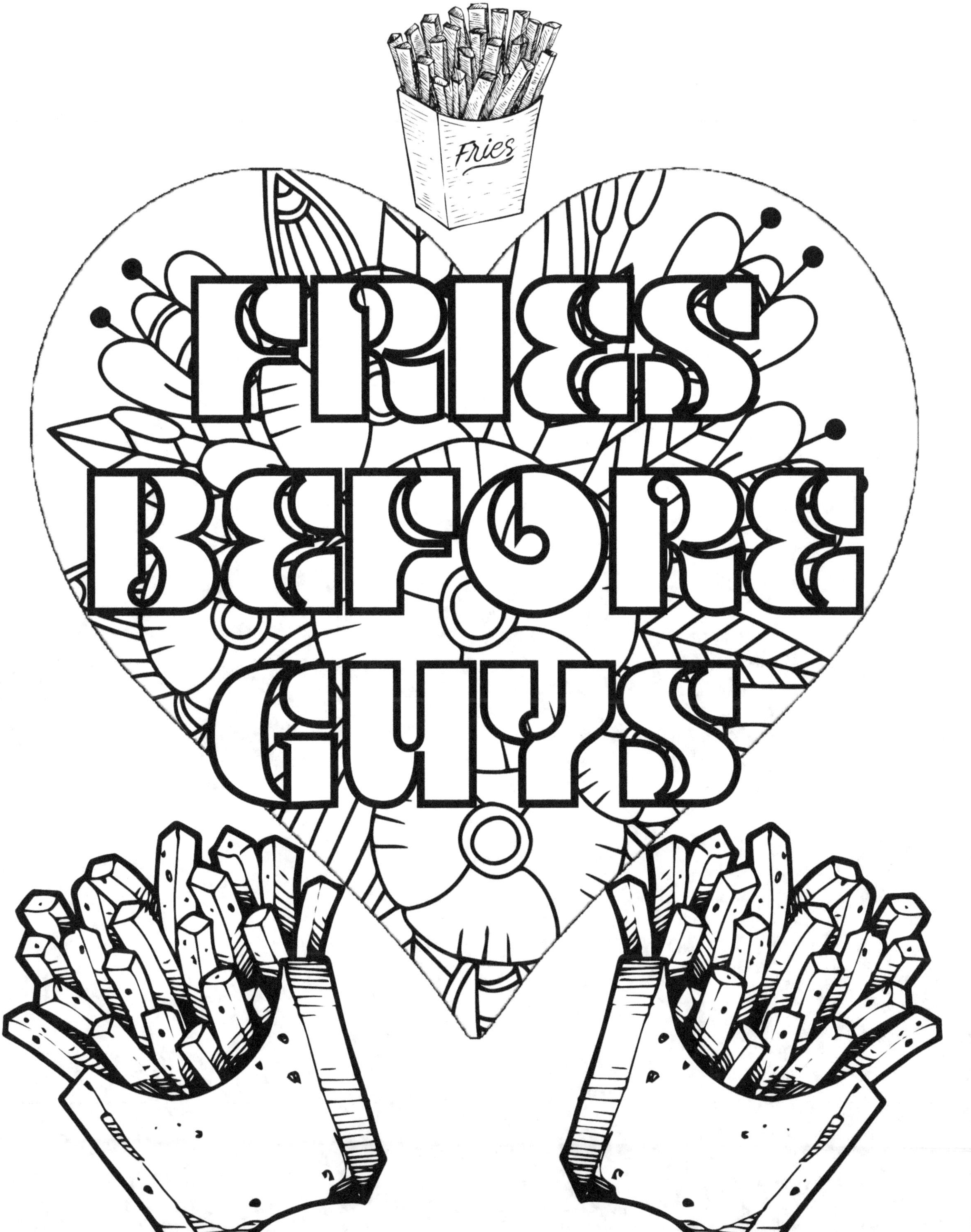
Fries
FRIES
BEFORE
GUYS

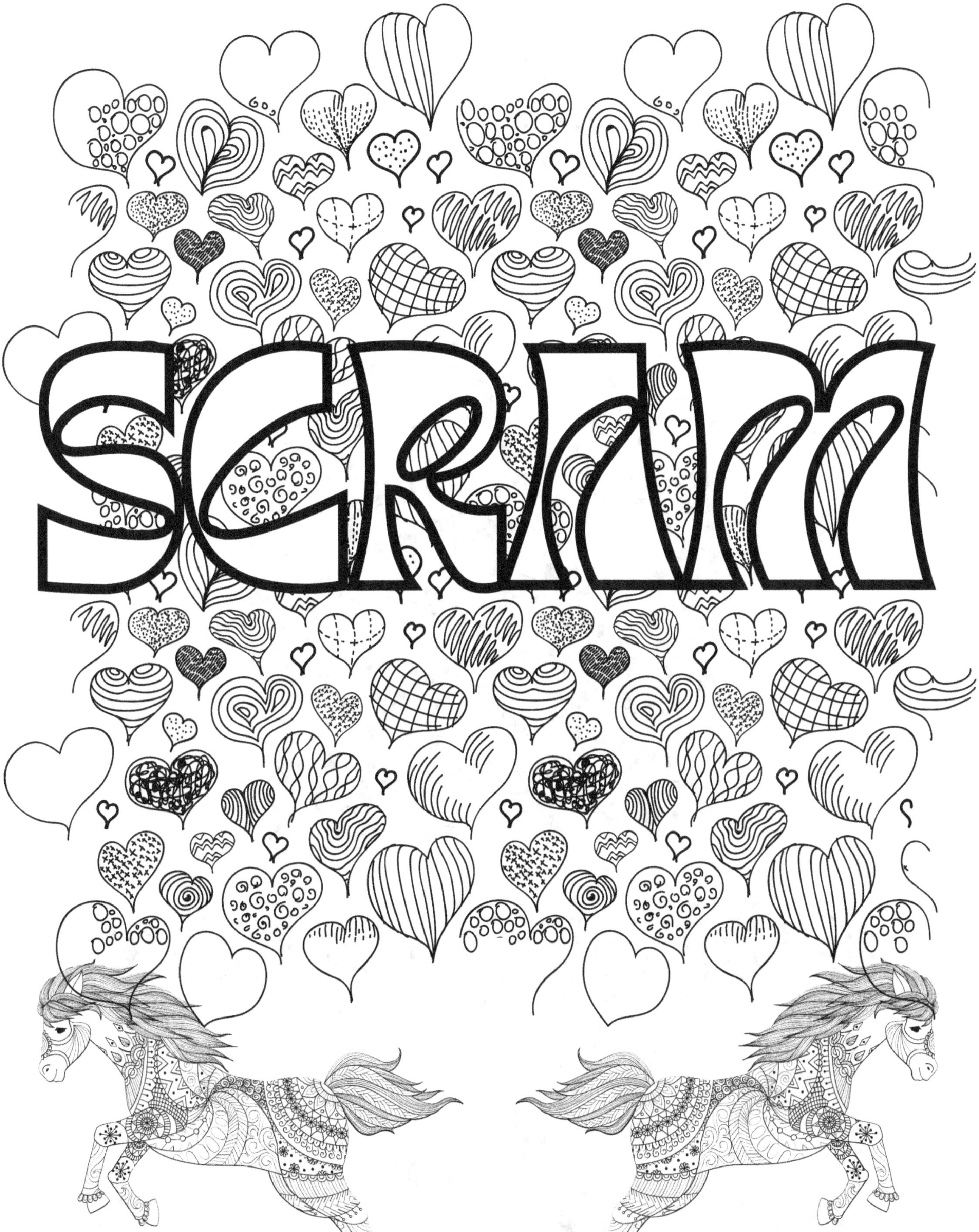
SCRAM

LIKE IT?

PLEASE CONSIDER RATING IT!

www.ingramcontent.com/pod-product-compliance
Lightning Source LLC
Chambersburg PA
CBHW080436220526
45465CB00019B/2336